Cultural Conflict and Adaptation: The Case of Hmong Children in American Society

Henry T. Trueba
Lila Jacobs
Elizabeth Kirton

The Falmer Press

(A member of the Taylor & Francis Group)
New York • Philadelphia • London

UK   The Falmer Press, Rankine Road, Basingstoke,
Hampshire RG24 0PR

USA   The Falmer Press, Taylor & Francis Inc., 1900 Frost Road,
Suite 101, Bristol, PA 19007

© H. T. Trueba, L. Jacobs, E. Kirton, 1990

First published 1990

British Library Cataloguing in Publication Data

Trueba, Henry T.
  Cultural conflict and adaptation: the case of Hmong children in
  American society.
  1. United States. Hmong children. Cultural identity
  I. Title   II. Jacobs, Lila   III. Kirton, Elizabeth
  305.2′3′0899591

ISBN 1-85000-761-6
ISBN 1-85000-762-4

Library of Congress Cataloging-in-Publication Data

Trueba, Henry T.
  Cultural conflict and adaptation: the case of Hmong children in
  American society/Henry T. Trueba, Lila Jacobs, Elizabeth
  Kirton.
  Includes bibliographical references.
  ISBN 1–85000–761–6: — ISBN 1–85000–762–4 (pbk.)
  1. Hmong American children—California. 2. Hmong
  Americans–California—Cultural assimilation. 3. Children of
  immigrants–California—Education. 4. Hmong American
  children. 5. Hmong Americans—Cultural assimilation.
  6. Children of immigrants—United States—Education.
  I. Jacobs, Lila. II. Kirton, Elizabeth. III. Title.
  F855.2.H55T78 1990
  305.23′089950792—dc20   89–29133
                                               CIP

Typeset in 11/13 Garamond by
Chapterhouse, The Cloisters, Formby L37 3PX

Jacket design by Benedict Evans

*Printed in Great Britain by Taylor & Francis (Printers) Ltd,
Basingstoke*

Contents

Acknowledgments

The authors feel profoundly grateful to the Hmong families, especially the children who permitted us to learn about their lives and experiences before coming to the United States and after their arrival. We feel respect and admiration for their courage and tenacity. We also want to thank the teachers, principal and all personnel from La Playa Elementary School (whose real names should remain unknown). Their help and understanding made possible our observations and interviews.

Each of the authors has many people to thank for their support and patience during the long hours of work preparing this manuscript. The support system, first at the University of California in Santa Barbara, later at the University of California in Davis is greatly appreciated.

Lila Jacobs wants to express her gratitude to the Graduate School of Education and the Social Process Research Institute at the University of California in Santa Barbara.

Elizabeth Kirton's valuable contributions to this volume, especially in matters that require accurate knowledge of the literature and a good understanding of the Hmong language, are particularly visible in Chapter 3 (La Playa Community). She is indebted to the Hmong community and the Wenner Gren Foundation for Anthropological Research whose support made it possible for her to conduct her doctoral dissertation research at the University of California, Santa Barbara.

Introduction: Significance of the Study

For many people around the world, the United States continues to represent the quintessence of contemporary democratic systems in the Western world. United States' history and reputation have been built on democratic ideals of equal opportunity for all that have attracted immigrants and refugees from all over the world. At the same time, however, many mainstream Americans view the arrival of new immigrants and refugees as a threat to political cohesiveness, domestic prosperity and peace. This perceived threat is linked to people's experience of cultural value conflict, economic competition, misunderstandings in communication, apprehension, and often prejudice. But, despite the perception of threat, the collective American ideal of being a host country for the people seeking political and religious freedom persists in the midst of controversy and opposition in the communities targeted for resettlement, and becomes interwoven with American cultural values stressing success, entrepreneurship and generosity.

Who are the Hmong people? Will the Hmong assimilate and become another success story? If so, how soon and at what price? What is the role of the school in the process of assimilation of the Hmong? Can school make this process more effective and less painful by helping Hmong children to integrate conflicting cultural values? This book attempts to answer these questions.

The Hmong people, with a total population of about 5 million, have a long history of statelessness and migration. During the last century, groups of Hmong moved from southern China (where 5 million Hmong still live) into Indochina, settling in Burma, Vietnam, Laos, and Thailand. As war refugees they have come to America in the last thirteen years. Many of the Hmong living in Indochina became involved in the Vietnam War, and some of them who had been associated with the American forces were invited to come to the United States as refugees when the Communists took control of Vietnam and Laos. It is calculated that approximately 90,000 Hmong refugees have come to this country, mostly to the states of Minnesota and California, and probably another 60,000 wait in camps along the Mekong River in the border between Laos and Thailand, hoping to join their relatives in the United States.

The Hmong (called Miao in mainland China) have the fame of being fierce fighters and mountain people with strong patrilineal clan. Traditionally Hmong grew rice as a subsistence crop and sometimes opium as a cash crop in the highlands. They also practiced animistic rituals, such as geomancy (search of sacred places for burial and eternal residence of clan members). Their courage as secret army soldiers working for the Central Intelligence Agency won them universal recognition. Between 1965 and 1975 about 30,000 were estimated to have died in the Vietnam War.

The latest statistics (1988) show about 59,000 Hmong people living in California, with half of them living in the Fresno area (Yang and North, 1988: 9). No longer the homogeneous group they were traditionally, Hmong now differ as to religion, education, and resettlement experience. Younger Hmong people begin to internalize American values and to put distance between themselves and their older family and clan members.

Between 1975 and 1985, the year in which we started this study, a small group of 426 (ninety households) came to live in La Playa, in west central California, their continuous migrations now part of the massive refugee movement. After surviving the wars, hunger, poverty and relocation traumas, these rugged people became well known in La Playa for their resourcefulness in adapting to a new environment.

The conversion of some Hmong to Christianity and the many cultural changes accompanying their new life have not affected the older generation's profound commitment to their language and culture. They are tough people, confident in facing the challenges of their new country. Yet, the older generations often feel nostalgic, insecure and uncertain about the future. They are aware that their cultural isolation is accentuated by the rapid erosion of Hmong language and cultural values among the school-age children. Grandparents recall with sadness a way of life that is now lost to them. They know the price they have paid for uprooting their families, and feel guilty for having abandoned relatives.

The anxiety suffered during their residence in the refugee camps of Thailand has not ended altogether. The ordeal of the war years, and of their exile, resettlement and relocation experiences, seem to be fresh in the minds of the senior generation.

Life for the Hmong in this country has not been easy either. The task of bringing and placing Hmong and other refugees was left to resettlement workers who had little time and training for coordinating massive efforts. The placement of refugees was disorganized and often conducted with painfully confusing or even contradictory policies. The result of these policies was long separations of close relatives and family members, and a phenomenon called 'secondary migration' which made it still more difficult to prepare, place and retain refugees upon arrival in this country. At the Thailand resettlement camps, and under enormous pressure, Hmong refugees had to investigate, compare and select sites for relocation offered by various voluntary agencies (such as the American Council for Nationalities Services, International Rescue Committee, and US Catholic Conference) in different countries, without fully understanding their rights and degrees of freedom in the potential locations of the available host countries. Naturally, soon after their arrival in this country, many Hmong people would start searching for relatives, then would assess their options, and make joint decisions with them to relocate where freedom and opportunity looked best — freedom to travel and use government stipends in any way they felt appropriate, and economic opportunity in the form of employment or welfare benefits. Secondary migrations, albeit costly, painful and often disappointing, tended to continue. Family reunification, lack of employment, high cost of living, hostility on the part of the host community, and intransigence on the part of sponsoring church organizations, were the key motivating factors of secondary and even tertiary migrations.

The Hmong confronted their problems and disappointments with little public complaint, showing the strength of their personality and the power of physical endurance that characterize their folk heroes. History and folklore come together in the daily lives of the Hmong, but more so as they uproot themselves and move to another place. The folktales, songs and historical accounts celebrating the virtues and heroic deeds of Hmong ancestors, the love of the family and loyalty to one's own kin, have for centuries helped the Hmong maintain a strong collective identity formed by loyal and strong people. Folklore continues to be the cement that articulates a deep religious belief system with the motivation to face the hardships of day-to-day life.

Many Hmong children, born in this country or too small to remember the tragic episodes of their parents' exile and resettlement, find themselves today in a strange world of cultural transition. They want to belong with their own people, and at the same time, they want to become mainstream Americans. Their confusion and ambivalence stem from various sources; they feel stereotyped by mainstream Americans in the community and schools, and they feel culturally isolated from both their home culture and the mainstream culture. In school they cannot talk about their cultural traditions to Americans who would not understand them. At home they cannot talk about school activities, because their parents do not understand them. Furthermore, Hmong children are rapidly losing their mother tongue; they hear and speak English all day long in school, and when they go home they watch TV in English.

Anthropologists have long collected and analyzed folklore because they see in it a reflection of the cultural values, social organization, myths and religious beliefs which form the fabric of daily life in societies. Folklore is a small window into the peculiar interpretation of the world that a group of people has shared and transmitted from generation to generation.

Although there are scholarly collections of Hmong folktales (most notably the volume edited by Johnson, 1985), we looked closely at a volume of folktales collected by a local teacher, Jean W. Cox (who admits not knowing the Hmong language) and Sheng Yang, one of her students who learned them from her father. This collection is entitled *Traditional Tales of the Hmong People* (Yang and Cox, 1985). Sheng Yang, now a teenager, remarks that in Laos when she was 5 years old, her father told her these stories before he died. Sheng views these stories not as fairy tales, but as accounts of what really happened many years ago. The stories depict family relationships and the triumph of traditional values.

The value of family relationships and the appropriate ways of handling interpersonal conflict are reflected, for example, in the story *How Goats Got Their Horns Twisted*. Here are some excerpts:

> A long time ago, there was a husband and wife. Every day the husband went out hunting animals, and every day his wife would bring lunch to him. Now, the husband was a good hunter, but he never shared what he killed with his wife: he ate it all himself. One day when his wife was bringing him lunch, she saw her husband eating a bird he had killed . . . The wife wrapped up her baby, and she left her baby and her husband. She returned to the water she had come from . . . All the household animals followed her because they were hers when she married. She went into the water up to her waist. 'Please come back wife . . . Come back and I will share with you from now on.' So the husband grabbed one of the goats by its head to pull it out of the water, and the wife grabbed the goat to pull it deeper into the water. They pulled and pulled until the goat had two twisted horns coming out of its head (Yang and Cox, 1985: 3).

Sharing and loyalty are extremely important values. The struggle of women who are unfairly treated by their husbands and the potential consequences for the husband if the wife goes away, portray the strong foundations of the Hmong family unit. The story is a warning and a reaffirmation of the cultural value placed on family stability.

Long-term commitment and the pursuit of love in the midst of war and chaos are illustrated by the story of the *The Poor Boy and the Dragon's Daughter*. The story depicts a poor boy, orphaned and unwanted in the village, who goes to the mountains. One day, in the mountains he hears his mother's voice 'My son, you must go to the lake'. Sheng Yang continues the story:

> When the poor boy got to the lake, he started to fish. Meanwhile, the daughter of the dragon who lived in the lake changed herself into a goldfish. The poor boy caught her, and when he caught her, the dragon's daughter changed into a beautiful woman (Yang and Cox, 1985:4).

The daughter of the dragon tells the boy: 'My father is sick. A fishing hook tore his mouth . . . If you help my father, I will marry you.' The boy went underwater and up into a dry cave where he found the sick dragon and cured him. The dragon told the boy: 'If you want to marry my daughter come back in two years and she will be a beautiful lady again.' The boy went back to the mountains, and in the meantime the dragon's daughter was taken prisoner by a king from the north. The boy went north, 'took off his ring and gave it to a serving girl to give to the dragon's daughter'. Then she knew that the boy still loved her. But the son of the king also wanted to marry the beautiful dragon's daughter. The story goes:

> To decide who would marry her, two tubs of boiling water were brought out. The one who loved her truly would not be harmed. Both the king's sons and the poor boy jumped into the boiling water, but it was the poor boy who came out, grown up, with new clothes and lots of money. The poor boy who was now rich and the dragon's daughter were married. They were very happy together (Yang and Cox, 1985: 4).

The test of true love is commitment and endurance through time and hardships. Love is rewarded by eternal happiness. Hardships are related to a violent takeover by powerful forces from the north. The loss of a lover, separation imposed by captivity, and the ultimate triumph of persistence and sacrifice mirror the story of many Hmong families and the cultural values that remain through the horror of war and poverty. The end of the story is unique. The boy is transformed by love and sacrifice into a mature man; with maturity he receives riches and happiness. The socialization of boys to endure pain and pursue long-term goals is cleary outlined in this story. In this story the sexual differentiation of roles is symbolized by the captivity of the beautiful dragon's daughter and her sacrifice in exchange for her father's health.

Women's role however has various nuances in the stories. The virtues that are extolled are obedience to the parents, tolerance and patience. There is a folktale entitled *The Boy with the Fat Stomach*, that illustrates the virtues admired in women. There was a king who owned many acres of rice fields and who had three beautiful daughters. There was a fat boy who was poor and an orphan, whose job was to watch the king's rice so that the birds wouldn't eat it. One day the boy shouted at the birds, 'I am poor. My job is to watch the rice!' The birds decided to help the boy by magically making him slim and dressing him with clothes of many colors, like the rainbow:

> The king told his oldest daughter to take food to the boy, but she said, 'No, I don't want to. He is fat, and I don't like him.' So the king told his middle daughter to take food to the boy, but the middle daughter said, 'No, I don't want to. He is fat, and I don't like him.' Finally the youngest daughter said, 'Father, I will take food to the boy.' And she did. She saw that he was handsome now, and she brought him home to her father, the king. Now the oldest daughter and the middle daughter saw the boy, and they wanted to marry him; but he said, 'No.' Then the oldest daughter and the middle daughter wanted to kill the youngest daughter so that the boy would marry [one of] them. Before this could happen, the king said, 'whoever took food to the boy will marry him.' This was the youngest daughter, Yer, so it was she who married the boy (Yang and Cox, 1985: 17).

The virtues of the youngest daughter were rewarded. This story is the Hmong version of Cinderella with a peculiar cultural twist. It relates a powerful message to girls that the virtues of tolerance, compassion and obedience are rewarded by marriage and happiness, and it warns them of the consequences of arrogance and intrigue. The head of the family, the king, comes across as a powerful figure with total control of what goes on within the family.

A theme often touched in folktales is the rivalry among sisters who are competing for a prospective bridegroom. *The Prince Snake and the Three Sisters* is such a story, in which young women are taught obedience and discretion. The king, who is father of three princesses, orders the first, then the middle and finally the youngest, to take care of a snake. The youngest daughter, the only one who obeys him, adopts the snake as a pet and goes with him to the ocean. The snake tells her, 'I'm going to jump into the water and colored bubbles will come up. Don't touch the yellow bubbles. Don't touch the green bubbles. But you can touch the red bubbles.' The narrative by Yang and Cox continues:

> But the youngest daughter did not listen. The snake jumped in and yellow bubbles came up. The girl did not touch them. Green bubbles came up, and — alas! — the girl touched them. The prince was not ready to come out, and instead her hand turned green and scaly. Then red bubbles came up, and the prince came out of the water. Now he was a handsome man and not a snake. The girl hid her green and scaly hand behind her. 'What is the matter?' the prince asked the girl. 'Nothing', she said, but the prince knew something was the matter. He looked at her hand and put it in the water; and when she took it out, it looked just like her other hand — normal. And she went home (Yang and Cox, 1985: 18).

But the story does not end here. The two older sisters became jealous of their younger sister and 'wanted to kill her and marry the prince'. The older sisters begged their younger sister to disclose the location in which she found her prince, because they also wanted the prince for themselves. The story goes on and finishes with an unexpected end:

> 'Go to the forest', the younger daughter told them, 'touch the first snake you see, and he will turn into a prince.' But the two older sisters saw a poisonous snake; and when they touched him they died (Yang and Cox, 1985: 18).

There are tragic results for the sisters who had attempted to kill their younger sibling and who had earlier disregarded their father's request to take care of the snake. Other stories of jealousy involve boys and kings, lies and virtues, but most of all, quick changes from poverty to riches.

Through Hmong folklore we have learned that the Hmong people are profoundly loyal to their families and committed to personal relationships. We have also learned that Hmong are long-term goal-oriented. They are willing to sacrifice comfort and good times in order to secure a long-term relationship with a person they love. The stability of the family is placed above other values. Hmong people truly believe that those who remain loyal to personal relationships and sacrifice their life to this end will be rich and happy.

The power of oral cultural tradition is evident. Children have internalized much of their parents' cultural heritage through folklore, and with it, the anxiety for survival and the nostalgia for the homeland some of them never saw. In fact, some of these children who were born in this country pretend to have lived through the resettlement experiences of Thailand by 'reminiscing' incidents which they have heard from others: 'Remember when I was . . . ' Their mothers, in good humour and affectionate tone, keep reminding them, 'You were born here, you are American.' Laughing in turn, children insist they were not born here. In their hearts they know better; they know that they are American, and there is no point of cultural return. But Hmong heritage is becoming more distant and intangible for young children. In fact, children are becoming so American that their parents' language and lifestyle are increasingly less meaningful and attractive, and at times, even embarrassing. Children, for example, hide the fact that one of their relatives is a shaman (a prestigious position in Hmong culture), and they avoid conversations about beliefs in the spirits, parents' occupations, traditional ceremonies, and other touchy issues.

War veterans and their families feel abandoned and hopeless. Wartime crises and sudden departures from place to place while living in Indochina have permanently changed family lives for generations to come. Old Hmong people still have many open wounds. When talking about a parent, a child, a brother or sister left in Laos or Thailand, women get tears in their eyes and change the topic of conversation away from thoughts that are too painful to remember.

Younger Hmong seem, for the most part, better adjusted and happier in America. Some worked with American military and government representatives in Indochina when they were in their teens or early twenties, and they came in close contact with American cultural values. Thus, they came with some ability in English and are comfortable dealing with Americans. Among their own people they are considered 'the experts' on American culture, and among Americans as 'the experts' on Hmong culture. Indeed they are viewed as truly 'bicultural', and rightfully so. But the Hmong family, as a sociocultural and economic unit, has little contact with American families. Parents express the common concern that rapid acculturation of their young children through the influence of school and friends will increase the generational gap and sociocultural distance between family members.

In spite of these concerns and fears, older Hmong people maintain strong family ties and resist acculturative influences perceived as incompatible with Hmong ancestral values. At the heart of the cultural cohesiveness, which transcends geographic and historical boundaries, are the unique values shared by Hmong families. Ceremonies performed in observation of events in the life cycle (birth, marriage and death, for example) reaffirm traditional values. The social activities associated with these ceremonies emphasize family unity, respect for the elderly, marriage loyalty, self-sacrifice for the kin, clearly defined sex roles, long-term pursuit of dreams and goals, stoic and patient suffering during hard times, cooperative approach to resolving family conflict and economic problems, protection of the young from the influences of outside societies and most of all, family privacy.

The loss of the above values or their gradual erosion, which evidently is occurring among the young Hmong people who strive to become 'American' all the way, is a profound collective concern for many Hmong. Indeed, the American lifestyle, with its social norms and the independence of the young adults, conflicts with Hmong traditions. Marriage patterns, for example, must be kept secret. Traditional marriages, because of the youth of the bride, parental involvement, and brideprice paid to the bride's family violate either legal or generally accepted norms in the United States. Highly prestigious occupations, such as those of shamans and curers, are now viewed with suspicion by outsiders, especially by members of sponsoring church organizations. Ritual ceremonies that had for years played a crucial role in maintaining mental health must also be abandoned or kept in secret.

While the junior generation seems to accept these constraints as facts of life, the senior generation views them as intolerable burdens and a serious blow to their cultural identity. Old people feel hopeless in their attempts to maintain Hmong language and culture. Many in the community are struggling to establish literacy classes, record folktales, and preserve traditional music before this part of their cultural heritage is lost.

In the midst of their rapid adjustment to this country's mainstream culture, many Hmong children find themselves lost in school, feeling ambivalent about their self-worth and self-identity. They are growing up with the ambitions and dreams of success, competition and wealth, which are an integral part of the American dream. Concern for upward socioeconomic mobility shows in their increasing aggressive competitiveness to excel in school. It is expected that professional excellence and high prestige will become likely candidates to replace home values. For junior high school Hmong students, who are going through the crucial years of puberty in which cultural transition and value integration are extremely fast, the family is losing its significance as the center of activities and the source of self-esteem and self-pride.

Most Indochinese children are adjusting well in this country, and Hmong refugees will undoubtedly adjust as well. It is only a matter of time, and much will depend on the support given by schools. The question is, are the schools prepared to assist these children in transition? The influx of refugee and immigrant children has been steady and has concentrated in relatively few schools within specified areas. The impact, consequently, can be massive, and it may create a sense of chaos and helplessness for school personnel. Teachers, principals, and the general public begin to wonder if schools can indeed fulfill their mission of mainstreaming minorities. At times, in the face of bewildering manifestations of cultural conflict and of the academic failure of minorities, teachers tend to feel guilty, personally hurt and collectively unprepared. There are no clear, quick recipes to resolve problems that developed over a period of years. Teachers begin to wonder if the democratic fabric of the United States has begun to fall apart in the midst of uncontrolled flow of immigrants and refugees, particularly those from exotic cultures and lower socioeconomic strata. It would seem that what teachers need the most is a deeper understanding of the home culture, of the desire to adjust, and of the nature of cultural shock suffered by both children and their teachers.

If we look at the drop-out problem in schools having heavy concentrations of minority students and an increase in violence and disruptive behavior, we will realize that the problems faced by educational administrators are not only organizational and disciplinary. They are also problems in understanding the motivation, thinking processes and constraints of minority students. In brief, the lack of cultural understanding contributes to the deep sense of frustration and resentment in teachers and administrators working with minority students. There is a cultural conflict and an emotional climate leading to misinterpretation of behavior, racial prejudice and almost despair. This climate does not permit systematic and rational instructional planning, much less the implementation of effective instructional activities. Indeed, some schools in the United States show urgent need for intervention. A concerted effort on the part of educational researchers, school administrators, community representatives and students themselves may still salvage instructional effectiveness and prevent the socioeconomic marginalization of minority students.

The sad reality of school districts impacted by the unexpected arrival of large numbers of ethnically diverse minority students is one of neglect and cultural insensitivity, of shock and anger on the part of both school personnel and students. Most of all, it is a waste of human talent and disregard for human dignity. Teachers and principals alone cannot change the institutional ways of dealing with new immigrants and refugees. This reality of ethnic diversity, cultural shock and rapid sociocultural change has yet to be taken seriously by higher education institutions responsible for teacher education programs and the supervision of pedagogical practices. It is precisely in this context that we decided to write this book as a contribution to awaken teachers, teacher educators and researchers to the sad and incongruent facts of multi-ethnic schooling.

This book reflects the thinking of professional educators and university faculty who are deeply involved in schools. We are concerned with problems of educational equity, instructional effectiveness and cultural sensitivity for the diverse ethnic groups represented in public schools. La Playa, an interethnic community located in the backyard of a major campus of the University of California, was chosen as an ideal location for our study. La Playa had been chosen as a resettlement area for various Indochinese refugee populations beginning in 1975.

The La Playa community was, and still is, composed of a relatively small group of permanent residents, low-income transient Anglos, students, a large Mexican community of undocumented workers with their families, and, since 1975, a large Indochinese population. The introduction of the refugees was but one more chapter in the local history of student protests, demonstrations, social disobedience, and other activities viewed as highly disruptive by the nearby campus administration. Even in this somewhat liberal environment, the arrival of the Hmong sent alarm signals to the Anglo members of the community, the homeowners, and the owners of apartment complexes.

The La Playa Elementary School, having seen several shifts in the local population, was taken by surprise once again in 1975 by the arrival of refugees from Laos, Cambodia, and Vietnam. Indeed the surprises continued from year to year because of the changes in student population, the arrival of new Indochinese, and an increase in children of foreign students at the university. At the time of the study in 1985–1986, the following twenty-four different language groups were represented in the La Playa school (presented from largest to smallest number of speakers): Spanish, Hmong, Lao, Vietnamese, Mandarin, Cantonese, Portuguese, Japanese, Hebrew, Arabic, Korean, Danish, Hindi, Croatian, Hungarian, Indonesian, Bengali, Dinka, French, Ilocano, Tagalog, Malaysian, Polish, and Punjabi.

We three authors had our children in the school for years and have worked cooperatively with the principal, teachers, counselors, and students since 1982 as aides, translators, and consultants. We are deeply involved in community-university relations and have followed the drama of several refugee and immigrant families whose children had problems at home or in school. During these years, we have been equally committed to traditional ethnographic field-based research. The more we knew about the school, the more we kept asking the same questions over a period of several years: Why do some children find school so difficult and incomprehensible while others adjust easily? Why do some teachers view minority children as incompetent, dumb, hopeless and unattractive? Why do so many minority children end up being classified as 'learning disabled'? What is the nature of such disabilities? What can the school do to help children and their families adjust?

When the school principal called on us for help, we just could not turn him down. He had tried everything and nothing seemed to work. We agreed to look into some of the most difficult cases and to help explain to the school personnel our opinion of the problems and potential solutions. We warned him, however, that we did not feel we could offer a quick remedy, or even a sure solution. This book gathers some of the data collected on one of the populations that was overrepresented among 'learning disabled' or 'problem children'. It attempts to answer some of the above questions with respect to the Indochinese refugees, especially the Hmong. We decided to write on the Hmong because they probably are the least known among all the Indochinese refugees coming from Laos, Cambodia and Vietnam. This is understandable in view of the fact that the Hmong had a long history as a minority, were viewed as a low-status group or a tribal people, and had been uprooted time and time again in their slow journey from northern China to Indochina and finally to Thailand. A second reason is that the role of the Hmong in the Vietnam War was secret, never clearly recognized in public by the United States. Hmong people were among the least conspicuous aides hired by the Central Intelligence Agency (CIA) during the covert operations conducted in Vietnam and Laos, when the Hmong General Vang Pao offered the American forces his support. A third reason is that the Hmong were usually grouped together with other ethnic Indochinese subgroups, such as the ethnic Lao, Cambodian and Vietnamese.

The Hmong people, however, did play a crucial role during the involvement of the United States Army in patrolling the Laotian jungle. When the United States Army withdrew its troops from Laos, top-ranking Hmong officers received offers of asylum in the United States. Other Hmong people were left to the mercy of the Pathet Lao, communist forces that had gained control of Laos in 1975. The Hmong people who had helped the Americans were seen by the new Laotian government as traitors, even in the cases when they had been forced to cooperate with the American forces. In order to avoid torment and death, many Hmong began their painful exodus through Laos to the border with Thailand. Walking through the jungle, usually at night and carrying young children and some of their belongings, they experienced a long, exhausting, and dangerous journey. Crossing the perilous Mekong River was indeed an unforgettable experience, and for some people, the last one. Numerous elder people, who had desperately struggled to reach safety and had it in sight, were physically exhausted and would die. Every family had its own history of tragedy, anxiety, loss of family members and possessions, terror of the enemy and unexpected close encounters with death.

When the Hmong finally arrived at the refugee camps in Thailand, they had hopes of leaving behind all hardships and of finding peaceful relocation in the United States or another wealthy Western country. Instead they discovered that communication with representatives from the United Nations High Commission on Refugees, the U.S. Government and voluntary agencies was extremely difficult. Many factors contributed to the problems in communication. Post-traumatic stress, confusion about resettlement policies, and other problems were compounded by the difficulty of making decisions without understanding the options available. These decisions were made primarily to comply with relocation requirements. At times, Hmong people had to acquire new identification documents purchased from other refugees, thus changing their names and their relationships. Some had to reclassify second wives and other relatives, pretending to be in full agreement with religious and cultural traditions imposed on them by church organizations and the U.S. Government. Most of all, they had to be interrogated again and again in order to prove that they had been associated with the American forces. To determine this fact, they were asked questions about the use of specific weapons; at times they had to explain why their assistance to Americans had not exposed them to any of those weapons. They were asked questions about people with whom they had not worked, American organizations with which they were not familiar, and operations in which they did not participate. The stress level was very high, since so much depended on the answers being satisfactory. Making the situation more tense was the fact that most Hmong could not communicate well, if at all, in English.

The increasing demand for relocation from large numbers of refugees was compounded by bureaucratic inefficiency and ethnocentrism. Family disagreements, stress, and conflict increased. As time passed, fewer options were available. Decisions to leave spouses' relatives in Thailand, or to accept relocation in unknown places added to their uncertainty and pain. At the root of the phenomenon of secondary and tertiary migrations in the host country was the lack of resettlement policies which were well-coordinated, consistent across organizations, and thoroughly explained to refugees.

The lack of information about the resettlement areas mirrored the ignorance about refugees on the part of mainstream community members in the host countries. Schools, surprised by the arrival of large numbers of refugees, were totally unprepared. Teachers who had no previous knowledge of the culture or language of the Hmong were expected to teach these children effectively. In La Playa the situation was becoming chaotic. From just a few children in 1980, the Hmong student population had increased to seventy-seven in 1986, becoming the second largest, following the 101 Mexican student population. The Hmong constituted 56% of the Indochinese student population, 27% of the minority population, and 13% of the entire student population in the La Playa school. Teachers felt unprepared to change their teaching style and curriculum in order to accommodate the newcomers. How did the new students behave in class? What was the quality of their work? How did teachers adjust to the new student composition? How did the families of these children adjust to the new culture, and how much support were they able to give their children for academic activities? How did school personnel deal with the problems of communication with the Hmong children and their families? How aware were teachers and children of the underlying cultural conflict, miscommunication, false expectations, stereotyping of the other group, and overall need to cooperate?

This book attempts to answer some of these questions. It will describe the journey of the families who lived in La Playa at the time of the study. The data, theoretical discussion and overall philosophy of this volume are presented in a concise and simple style, with an optimistic view of the future. We are aware that schools are growing increasingly less humane and tolerant of cultural differences, and that minority children are becoming more isolated and less rewarded. We work closely with teachers in ethnically diverse schools and have come to realize that even those among them who are well prepared and deeply committed to their careers find teaching frustrating, not effective, constrained and confining. Many teachers burn out before they see the positive results of their hard labor. Probably most teachers are eager to face school problems and search for solutions with honesty and determination, but they do not know how to organize their efforts.

This book is intended to help educators peek through the small window of our descriptions and theoretical discussions into the world of Hmong and other minority children who are making desperate efforts to belong in American society, to achieve and to be loved for their accomplishments. As educators get a glimpse of the family life and painful experiences of the Hmong people, they will find some insights into the nature of cultural conflicts in ethnically diverse schools. The challenge of facing and resolving cultural conflicts is difficult, but when viewed in someone else's school, it helps reflection and understanding.

The appreciation and respect for one's own culture constitute the foundations for the respect and appreciation of other peoples' culture. We could echo St Augustine's expressions and apply them to minority children's culture:

> Sero te amavi, pulchritudo tam antiqua et tam nova, sero te amavi! Et ecce intus eras et ego foris, et ibi te quaerabam... Mecum eras, et tecum non eram. (Late I came to love you, beauty so old and so new, late I came to love you! You see, you were inside of me and I was out, and I was looking for you out there... You were in me, and I wasn't with you (St Augustin's Confessions in Custodio Vega, 1963).

Chapter one

Culture Conflict and the American Dream

American society has been historically pluralistic and uniquely creative in confronting cultural conflict and adapting to change resulting from cultural diversity. Conflict has led to successful integration of values and an enriched understanding of democracy.

Minorities and Democracy

Without the contributions, loyalty and extraordinary energy of the incessant waves of immigrants from all over the world, American democracy would have long ceased to exist. Immigrants and refugees come to America searching for economic opportunities and political and religious freedom, 'The American Dream'. No one else knows better than the immigrants and refugees the meaning of freedom and democracy, and no one is willing to pay a higher price in order to achieve the American dream. Therefore they endure hardships and drastic social and cultural changes unbearable for others, and they buy into American ideals of social, economic and political participation, and of educational opportunity equally accessible to all. Indeed they learn that the very foundations of American democratic institutions are linked to the reality of ethnic diversity and the eager dedication of newcomers to succeed (Spindler, 1977, 1987; Spindler and Spindler, 1983, 1987a, 1987b; DeVos, 1982; Suarez-Orozco, 1989; Trueba, 1989; Delgado-Gaitan, 1989). Educators, especially teachers, need to become aware of the contributions of immigrants and refugees to America in order to inculcate in all students genuine appreciation for the richness of American culture and of immigrants' commitment to the continued existence of democratic institutions.

Immigrant and refugee families' success, however, depends much on their ability to overcome the cultural conflicts associated with drastic culture changes, that is, with their flexibility to acquire new beliefs, codes of behaviour, and communication patterns, and their ability to handle stress

1

and prejudice. It is precisely in this context that the work of educators takes special significance; educators become the key agents of socialization of culturally-different children (Delgado-Gaitan, 1987a, 1987b; Hornberger, 1988; Borish, 1988; Trueba, 1983, 1987a, 1987c, 1988a, 1988b, 1988c, 1989). Beyond their obligation to transmit knowledge, teachers are the role models of American democracy, the cultural brokers in charge of helping all children internalize new cultural knowledge and values that are congruent with our social, political and economic organizations.

Refugee and immigrant children cannot succeed in American society without understanding the American system, its institutional organization and its philosophy. The acquisition of the English language is crucial to their adjustment to our society, their acceptance of new values and their participation in public life. How can one expedite the acquisition of English? What instructional and language policies, what educational philosophy and classroom activities can maximize the learning of English by new students? Recent publications have addressed these issues. Social, demographic and economic factors do affect English literacy acquisition. Low literacy levels in English tend to be associated with cultural conflicts, isolation and poverty (Trueba, 1987a, 1987b; Goldman and Trueba, 1987; Trueba and Delgado-Gaitan, 1988; Trueba, 1988a, 1988c, 1989).

Role of Schools in the Education of Minorities

Some neighborhoods and schools have become overwhelmed by the rapid influx of refugee, immigrant, ethnolinguistic minority and low-income families. The isolation of these families and their children prevents them from engaging in the process of adapting to American society and acquiring the skills necessary to share in the benefits that society offers to newcomers. School administrators, teachers, and social scientists see the lack of English literacy as the roots of disempowerment and one of the most serious problems that American society has yet to face (Spindler, 1977, 1987; Spindler and Spindler, 1983, 1987a, 1989; Giroux, 1983; Giroux and McLaren, 1986; Shulman, 1987a, 1987b; Sockett, 1987).

One of the consequences of illiteracy is low achievement in school. Researchers have not been able to explain adequately why some immigrant, refugee and minority groups achieve in school at higher levels than others. Some pseudo-researchers have presented controversial explanations based on genetic factors (Jensen, 1981; Dunn, 1987). The reaction from social scientists has been unequivocal in rejecting such a position (see Trueba, 1988d, and responses). In contrast, cultural ecologists (Ogbu, 1974, 1978,

1987a, 1987b) argue that social, psychological and cultural factors explain the differential achievement of some groups. Attempts have been made to analyze these explanations and to provide supportive and complementary arguments (Trueba, 1986, 1987a, 1987c, 1988a, 1988b, 1988c, 1989) in order to consider the implications of theory for educational practice.

According to some researchers the ethnic culture plays a similar role in both successful learning and the 'social accomplishment' of academic failure (Florio-Ruane, 1988). That is particularly true of the ultimate failure of dropping out and rejecting educational institutions, their knowledge, norms and values.

While cultural ecologists have made important contributions to our understanding of differential minority achievement, their indiscriminate use and application of minority group taxonomies (designations of caste-like, autonomous, and immigrant types) for entire ethnic or minority groups has theoretical and political consequences that are unacceptable (Trueba, 1988b: 271–287). These taxonomies are based on theories of differential school achievement which do not allow for either individual or collective change in status, and therefore tend to stereotype further some ethnic groups. Besides, these theories do not explain the transition from failure to success of some 'caste-like' minorities. 'Caste-like' minorities are described as follows:

> *Castelike* or *involuntary minorities* are people who were *originally brought into United States society involuntarily* through slavery, conquest, or colonization. Thereafter, these minorities were relegated to menial positions and denied true assimilation into mainstream society. American Indians, black Americans, and Native Hawaiians are examples. In the case of Mexican Americans, those who later immigrated from Mexico were assigned the status of the original conquered group in the southwestern United States, with whom they came to share a sense of peoplehood or collective identity (Ogbu, 1987b: 321; emphasis in original).

Is it historically defensible that all or most Mexican Americans were colonized or entered this country involuntarily, or that they have been denied the opportunity to become mainstream in America? On the contrary, there is evidence of fairly rapid acculturation of many who lose their language and culture. Many more continue to arrive of their own free will seeking economic and educational opportunities. In fact, some border authorities estimate an average of 3000 illegals cross the San Diego border every day. About 1000 of them are returned immediately to Tijuana, only to attempt again and again to move north.

Success or failure to learn are related to the acquisition of communication skills whose development is anchored in culturally congruent and meaningful social exchanges. Academic achievement or failure to achieve, more than an individual attribute, is a reflection of the sociocultural system which offers or denies a child the opportunity for meaningful social intercourse, and thus for cognitive development. As such, academic achievement is fully understandable only in its macro-historical, social, economic and political context. Academic success or failure are not caused by a single social institution, such as the school or the family (Cole and Griffin, 1983: 71), but by a whole set of institutions (religious, political and economic) which provide children with experiences that maximize or curtail cognitive development. In this sense, both academic success and academic failure are socially constructed phenomena:

> Working within pre-existing social norms and role relationships, teachers and students collaborate to create the linguistic and social conditions under which students fail to learn.... Misunderstandings of one another at that time can lead to assessment of students as less than able or interested learners (Florio-Ruane, 1988: 1).

Is academic knowledge acquired as easily and naturally as the concrete knowledge required to handle day-to-day social interactions and problem solving situations? Some researchers believe formal or taxonomic knowledge, that is, the knowledge taught in school, is no more difficult to acquire than the linguistic and cultural knowledge obtained through daily experiences. Thus, they reason, resistance to learning should be viewed as students' rejection of cultural values and academic demands placed on them by school personnel (Erickson, 1984). Is the academic underachievement of some minority students to be interpreted as resistance to the values advocated by mainstream students and faculty? In other words, are we dealing with the consequences of cultural conflict during the years of transition from the home to the school culture?

Culture Conflict and Learning

The assumption that culture and cultural conflict play a key role in the acquisition of second language literacy is confirmed by recent studies on

English literacy acquisition which have analyzed the use of culturally and linguistically congruent instructional approaches in order to smooth the transition from the home to the school learning environment. Examples of these analyzes are found in the following: Au and Jordan (1981) and Tharp and Gallimore (1989) in the Kamehameha Schools of Hawaii and southern California; Delgado-Gaitan (1987a, 1987b, 1989) with Mexican children in northern and central California and Trueba (1987c, 1988a, 1988c, 1989, 1990) with Hispanic and Indochinese. In contrast, other studies have shown the consequences of the use of instructional approaches which are culturally incongruent, for example, Richards (1987) among the Mayan children of Guatemala, Hornberger (1988) among the Quechua children of Peru, Macias (1987) among the Papago, and Deyhle (1987) among the Navajo. The significance of those studies is that the use of instructional models capitalizing on the minority children's home language and culture has positive results on their overall adjustment to school and society.

One way of becoming more sensitive to minority students' needs is the use of what George and Louise Spindler (1982) have termed *Reflective Cultural Analysis*. The Spindlers have consistently viewed education as a dimension of cultural transmission — implying the inculcation of specific cultural values. What *Reflective Cultural Analysis* can do is to reveal to educators their unconscious biases and cultural ethnocentrism in dealing with minority students.

Using cross-cultural comparisons, along the lines of the Spindlers' Reflective Cross-Cultural Interview (Spindler and Spindler, 1982, 1987a), Fujita and Sano (1988) have compared and contrasted American and Japanese day-care centers. They elicited and analyzed videotapes of Japanese and American teachers; then they asked one group of teachers to interpret the behaviors of the other group. This study has permitted authors and researchers to reflect on the ethnocentrism and projection of cultural values reflected in day-care activities. For the American it is a socialization for 'independence'. For the Japanese it is a socialization for 'tolerance and cooperation'.

Cross-cultural studies have also helped in understanding the cultural adaptations of subgroups within a larger society. Borish (1988), for example, looking at the academic socialization of young adults, adopts the Spindlers' model of 'compression and decompression' cycles and focuses on high school students in the Kibbutz as they get ready to enter the armed forces and endure intense manual labor experiences 'in the winter of their discontent.'

Cultural conflict has been studied by several anthropologists. DeVos, for example, has used projective techniques to explore the complex layers of personality structure and motivational processes in minority achievement (1967; 1973, 1980, 1982, 1983, 1984; DeVos and Wagatsuma, 1966; Wagatsuma and DeVos, 1984). Suarez-Orozco (1987, 1989), using cultural ecological approaches and projective techniques, shows how Central American refugee children succeeded academically due to their family loyalty. Their motivation to achieve was an expression of their profound commitment to assist and make proud their parents left behind in war-torn Central America.

Minority Groups in America

Upon examining the demographic distribution of language minority groups given in the 1980 Census data, as well as advance analysis of recent demographic data (U.S. Bureau of the Census, 1984; and U.S. Department of Commerce, 1987), the authors found that linguistic minority enrollment in our public schools will increase dramatically in the last decade of this century and in the following years. The future of American democracy, technological development, economic power and military power will be to a large extent in the hands of children whose mother tongue is other than English.

There are approximately 35 million persons in the United States who speak a language other than English at home, of whom about 20 million are not fluent in English. Almost 11 million of them are school-age children. Almost 50% of this linguistic minority population (about 16 million) are Spanish-speaking. Together, French, German and Italian speaking linguistic minorities make 8.4 million (or 24.2%). The Spanish-speaking population is concentrated in the southwestern states of California (7 million), Texas (3.8 million), Arizona (727,000), New Mexico (618,000), and Colorado (475,000) (U.S. Bureau of the Census, 1984; U.S. Department of Commerce, 1987).

The larger society is mirrored in the structure and composition of public schools which have become a futuristic microcosm of American society, and as such reflect the same biases and prejudicial attitudes towards minorities. School teachers and administrators are torn between the dilemma of American democratic ideals advocating educational opportunity for all, and the low expectations shared by most Americans of minority students' achievement. See, for example, Jensen (1981) and Dunn (1987) who argue that genetic constitution explains the lower achievement of Blacks and Hispanics. While these pseudo-scientists are not taken seriously by their colleagues, their work, nevertheless, has had a devastating

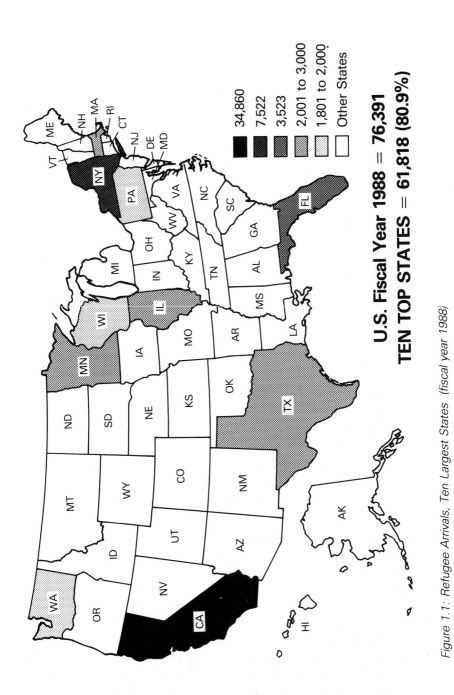

U.S. Fiscal Year 1988 = 76,391
TEN TOP STATES = 61,818 (80.9%)

34,860
7,522
3,523
2,001 to 3,000
1,801 to 2,000
Other States

Figure 1.1: Refugee Arrivals, Ten Largest States (fiscal year 1988)

Table 1.1 *Estimated Numbers of Language Minority People in the United States, by Age Group, English or Non-English Language Spoken at Home and Language: 1980 (numbers in thousands)*

Language	Total	Children <5[2]	People living in language minority families[1]						Other home speakers of NELs
			Aged 5–17			Aged 18 and older			
			Total	Speak English	Speak NEL	Total	Speak English	Speak NEL	
Total	34,637	2,562	7,948	3,466	4,482	20,616	5,549	15,067	3,511
Spanish	15,548	1,537	4,164	1,284	2,879	8,472	1,610	6,862	1,375
French	2,937	147	685	468	218	1,776	772	1,004	328
German	2,834	120	594	401	193	1,773	727	1,046	348
Italian	2,627	86	437	285	152	1,871	637	1,233	233
Polish	1,285	31	166	123	43	916	310	606	172
Chinese languages	769	58	152	37	115	476	44	432	84
Filipino languages	713	70	168	104	63	423	64	359	52
Greek	548	33	108	42	66	361	71	290	46
Japanese	542	26	98	65	33	358	114	244	59
American Indian or Alaska Native languages	512	54	155	66	89	262	59	203	41
Portuguese	480	34	103	36	67	307	57	249	35
Yiddish	430	16	41	22	20	290	76	214	83
Korean	384	40	95	36	60	224	42	182	25
Asian Indian Languages	321	41	67	24	43	188	12	175	25

Arabic	312	32	64	26	38	179	37	142	38
Hungarian	266	8	37	24	12	186	55	131	36
Dutch	252	13	52	36	16	159	54	105	27
Vietnamese	250	27	75	14	61	122	15	107	27
Russian	232	10	34	15	20	152	34	117	36
Serbo-Croatian	211	10	35	16	19	146	35	110	21
Czech	194	5	26	21	5	134	46	87	29
Norwegian	184	5	26	19	7	120	48	72	34
Ukrainian	168	6	22	12	10	121	28	92	19
Swedish	163	5	22	15	7	103	43	60	33
Slovak	141	2	15	12	3	106	40	66	19
Armenian	127	6	20	7	13	89	14	75	12
Persian	138	10	24	7	17	76	14	63	28
Thai	127	17	31	11	21	66	14	52	13
Finnish	111	3	16	13	3	74	26	48	19
Lithuanian	104	2	11	8	3	73	21	52	17
Other languages	1,726	108	404	216	188	1,015	428	587	198

NEL — a non-English language.

1 Families in which one or more family members speak a non-English language at home.

2 Children one or both of whose parents speak a language other than English at home.

Note: Detail may not add to total because of rounding.

Source: U.S. Bureau of the Census. (1984) *1980 U.S. Census* Current Populations Report, Washington, DC: Government Printing Office.

impact in some school districts. Jensen's and Dunn's misunderstanding of what tests mean is rooted in their disregard for cultural factors and rigid definitions of intelligence. From an anthropological perspective (DeVos, 1973, 1980; Spindler, 1977; Spindler and Spindler, 1983, 1987a; Cummins, 1986, 1989; Trueba *et al.*, 1984; Trueba, 1988a, 1988c, 1988d, 1989) intelligence is the ability to pursue individual and group cultural goals through activities perceived as enhancing the home culture values. Intelligence is definitely not measurable by the ability to score high in tests constructed by individuals from another culture in narrowly constructed literacy and problem-solving settings. Cultural anthropologists (DeVos, 1980, 1983; DeVos and Wagatsuma, 1966; Wagatsuma and DeVos, 1984; Ogbu, 1974, 1978, 1987a, 1987b; Gibson, 1987, and others) have documented the fact that the same ethnic group can achieve high scores in one country and low scores in another. The Koreans (DeVos, 1973), for example, who are collectively considered outcast in Japan and have the highest crime rates and the lowest academic achievement, are recognized as outstanding and law-abiding students in the continental U.S., Hawaii and Europe.

The treatment of immigrant and refugee children seems to vary from country to country and from place to place. Many immigrant and refugee children endure a life of poverty and rural isolation in crowded dwellings. Their families lack privacy, toilet and shower facilities, comfort, and basic medical attention. In some cases immigrant life for children means physical abuse, malnutrition, poor health, ignorance and educational neglect. For others, there is also a sort of cultural and linguistic isolation with respect to their own language and culture. They are unable to develop their cognitive skills and do not perform at levels comparable to those of mainstream students, and they are seen as 'educationally retarded', a label often leading to the stereotypic formal classification 'learning disabled'. Gradually they come to lack self-esteem and appreciation for their own culture. Consequently, they show low aspirations, and social and economic dependence on low-paying jobs.

This complex process of social stratification of minorities is linked to the painful experience of incompetence and shock in dealing with mainstream persons representing social institutions such as banks, hospitals, stores, recreation facilities, churches, businesses and service agencies. Adults often face serious difficulties in communicating in written and oral English with mainstream persons. Therefore, they depend on their own children for translation. This forces bilingual children into a position of adult responsibility in making economic, social, medical and other difficult personal decisions. In this context, we can better understand the deep anxiety of some immigrants and their parents in day-to-day interaction. Their suspicion of unfair treatment or even racism may simply be a misunderstanding of the red-tape characteristic of our institutions. It is tragic that these parents' feelings and views may create in children some hostility towards and misconception of cultural values.

Older immigrant and refugee children have burdens and responsibilities that their younger siblings rarely face. They often describe in realistic terms their experiences working in the fields, moving around the country, living in filthy rooms, and feeling humiliated in schools because of their appearance, smell and behavior. Some adult immigrants have bitter memories of their first day of school when their hair was washed with kerosene or was cut in front of their peers — an inhuman attempt to solve the lice problem in rural children. Others remember their peers calling them names or covering their noses because they smelled.

Cultural Values and Achievement in Schools

The debate over the concept of culture has continued for at least the past 120 years. It seems that the complexity and change inherent in any concepts of culture advanced recently have added fuel to the controversy. At the heart of the controversy is the application of the term to groups and social entities which are hardly comparable in terms of size, structural complexity, organization and self-sufficiency.

The Concept of Culture

Some social scientists have comfortably disregarded the pronouncements of early anthropologists as unclear or irrelevant. Others have decided to transcribe any traditional definition of culture appearing in textbooks and pay lip service to the presence of culture in the schools. The concept of culture and its application to American society is important and must be examined in a historical perspective.

Culture was defined by nineteenth century anthropologists as knowledge, beliefs, art, morals, law, custom, habits and capabilities acquired by members of a given society. At the beginning of this century anthropologists defined it as what is not determined genetically but learned socially, the 'social inheritance', including cultural and linguistic patterns of behavior. In the 1970s, Goodenough (1971) defined culture as a set of norms of behavior in the minds of individuals who share much of the content of those norms: the organization of their real and phenomenal world experiences; their belief system; and their overall taxonomic cognitive system shared with members of the same group.

In the 1980s the concept of culture has been changed in a significant way as it was applied to bodies of literature and specific theoretical contexts (Spindler and Spindler, 1983). D'Andrade (1984), for example, agrees with previous anthropologists who viewed culture as consisting at the very minimum of knowledge and codes of behavior being transmitted from one generation to the next. He feels, however, that 'most systems of meaning that are culturally acquired are not purely representational' (1984: 97), but that 'various elements of the meaning system come to have a directive force', and consequently, that 'the goals stipulated in the cultural meaning system are intrinsically rewarding'. D'Andrade means that 'through the process of socialization, individuals come to find achieving culturally prescribed goals and following cultural directives to be motivationally satisfying' and consequently that they find 'not achieving such goals or following such directives to be anxiety producing' (1984: 98).

Modern anthropologists, particularly those who have followed the discussion of culture for several decades, have come to the conclusion that ever since the beginning of anthropological tradition, anthropologists have recognized the relationship between behavior and cultural codes, and that the quintessence of culture is precisely determined by the nature of this relationship. The Spindlers, for example, see culture as consisting of organized activities one engages in to obtain possessions, recognition, power, satisfaction or other socially approved goals (Spindler and Spindler, 1987a and 1987b).

Changes in the concept of culture during the last three decades are in part the result of methodological reforms in the approach to the study of culture. Ethnography, which is the primary scientific tool in the study of culture, has been conducted by early anthropologists without the benefits of cross-cultural knowledge accumulated later, and without the focus and systematic rigor which were later borrowed from sociology, linguistics and psychology. Ethnography uses participant observation techniques as one of the main tools for gaining insight into the relationships between activity organization and cultural goals. The assumption is that if one observes social interaction long enough, one can, in the end, make inferences about cultural codes of appropriate behavior and will be able to reconstruct the meaning of symbolic systems. Because one cannot observe the lives of hundreds of people in detail, the second best method is to get information from those who are members of a given culture.

According to D'Andrade not all human phenomena can be considered to be organized into meaning systems. He goes a step further by suggesting that a relationship exists between meaning systems and the class of human phenomena not organized as meaning systems, which he calls 'material flow'. Material flow includes 'the movement of goods, services, messages, people, genes, diseases, and other potentially countable entities in space and time' (D'Andrade, 1984: 110). Economic, demographic and other particular characteristics of human groups, with their own laws and patterns of behavior, escape the taxonomy of meaning systems. Therefore, cognitively oriented definitions of culture do not do justice to the study of such complex phenomena. One of these phenomena is the differential learning outcomes of socioculturally different children in schools. In the study of culture it is important to explore the process of human adaptation to the environment, and how humans reorganize behavior, affect and thought through activities that promise the rewards emphasized by their cultural values.

The study of culture, both culture as a whole and culture of the schools, must adhere to certain principles in order to provide an accurate picture of people's views, values, behaviors and cultural codes. Suffice it to say that the study of cultural transmission (that is, of knowledge and cultural values), particularly through school activities, requires systematic observations, careful interviewing, and the use of well-crafted instruments. It also requires both cross-cultural and historical analytical frames of reference.

If America is composed by mainstream and minority persons, who is then mainstream, and who is minority? Can we choose our affiliation? Can we change our affiliation? What are the social consequences of belonging to the mainstream segment of American society? As in any ethnic or cultural groups, there seems to be a spectrum of differential membership and differential affiliation to minority groups that may extend to individuals only marginally associated with the minority group. Indeed we hold flexible operational definitions and criteria for ethnic identification, and we manipulate boundaries in diverse political contexts. Some individuals who have been active members of minority communities and clearly recognized as minority by outsiders, can switch group affiliation in certain contexts and feel and behave like members of the mainstream. At the same time, individuals who look as if they are mainstream, can switch cultural and linguistic codes and interact comfortably with the minority community from which they originated.

The work of the Spindlers (Spindler, 1977, 1987, 1987b; Spindler and Spindler, 1983, 1987a) would suggest that we consider a mainstream American person (regardless of ethnohistorical background) as one who:

1. Holds values traditionally viewed as 'American' (freedom to disagree, to assemble, working ethics, respect for other people's religion, etc.).
2. Speaks English fluently (with native-like oral skills).
3. Shares on the historical traditions, folklore and myths of Americans.
4. Participates actively in the American social, political, and economic life.
5. Seeks voluntarily affiliation with mainstream persons as an integral component of his/her cultural identity.

Can any ethnolinguistic minority group become part of the mainstream society? What determines the compatibility of cultures? What are the characteristics of the Hmong culture and to what extent is Hmong culture an obstacle to acculturation into mainstream American society?

Mainstream affiliation is the dream of most immigrants, but is becomes impossible when minority groups are kept in social, economic or political isolation. However, when minority, immigrant and refugee groups have free access to American mainstream society, they become members of mainstream society without cutting their ties with their original minority culture. This is obtained by becoming bilingual or even bicultural, and by acquiring the linguistic, cognitive and cultural knowledge and skills necessary to function effectively in mainstream public social settings.

Membership in either mainstream or minority groups tends to be ascribed by the casual observer on the basis of physical, linguistic (primarily phonetic) and superficial behavioral characteristics. Cultural ascription may be in conflict with cultural affiliation (one's own ethnic identity) as internalized by each individual. Collective perception of membership is particularly painful to individuals who share characteristics and cultures viewed as incompatible and resulting from intermarriages perceived as undesirable. For example, offspring of Southeast-Asian women and American men, called 'Amerasians', had a stigma and low status. The stigma was drastically reduced or even disappeared as these children were recognized as 'Americans' and accepted in the United States.

Schooling and Mainstreaming

The dramatic changes in American society, as reflected in the ethnic composition of the east and southwest populations and the occupational profile of the labor force, express a serious concern on the part of schools, which are responsible for mainstreaming immigrants and refugees. There is an increasing awareness of the need to develop the advanced academic training demanded by employers as a hiring requirement. Knowing what our parents learned in the 1930s and 1940s will not insure us a job sufficient to provide the necessary support for our families today. The percentage of the American population working in semi-skilled or unskilled jobs continues to decrease, and even the skilled laborers are now in competition with equally skilled people of other countries whose wages are a fraction of those of American workers.

The most important function of schools, that of socializing youth into American cultural values and preparing them to play a role in society, has become more demanding and difficult. School used to be a place where children acquired reading and writing skills, learned American history and literature, and prepared for membership in the labor force. Schools also had the function of mainstreaming immigrants and channeling them into the various openings in the labor market.

The first function of school, providing knowledge, has increased in amount and complexity. Chemistry, physics, anthropology, biology and genetics have not only advanced a great deal, but have also generated complex interdisciplinary sub-fields such as paleoanthropology, biogenetics, biochemistry, and nuclear physics. There are many more subjects that are far more complicated today than there ever were before.

The second function of schools, mainstreaming immigrant and minority students, was once limited to those who shared the same race and western culture. Other groups, such as Blacks and non-White minorities, were segregated in society and in school. With the Civil Rights Act of 1964 schools were pressed to become integrated. The contrast between the academic achievement of minorities in segregated schools and that of mainstream students was shocking and demanded changes towards educational equity. One of the drastic changes whose results are clear in today's public schools is the overall proportion of immigrant and minority students to mainstream students, and the enormous diversity of new-comers; socially, economically, culturally and academically diverse students are now sharing classrooms, yet they are instructed (or better, managed) with the same techniques and curricula used for mainstream children.

Acculturation and Achievement

Achievement is the expected outcome of teaching and learning and of the overall experience of schooling. However, the process of formal instruction is seen as the most essential requirement for academic achievement. This process is a two-way communication between teacher and student which goes beyond the transmission of content. Under the guidance of the teacher as representative of American social institutions, students are guided toward an understanding, acceptance and internalization of specific cultural values which constitute the very foundations for academic learning. These values, for example, affect the pre-literacy and literacy stages of academic achievement at the collective and individual levels. These values foster commitment to the use of text, the organization of information through text, the virtues of national heroes depicted in textbooks, the advocacy for values exemplified by the lives of historical figures, and the motivation to record through text, historical events which build national pride and political unity. These values are transmitted in school through multiple channels during the instructional process and the many extracurricular activities. Schools capture the quintessence of American culture and transfer it to students.

American culture plays a role even in the actual organization of the instructional process imparting academic instruction. Teaching requires the transfer of knowledge through linguistic and cultural codes familiar to students. Beyond academic knowledge, the communication of messages, norms of behavior and methodological strategies provided to students, so they develop their own knowledge base and cognitive skills, requires linguistic and cultural knowledge common to teachers and students.

The teacher's role consists primarily of facilitating the transmission of cultural values needed by students to become motivated to learn. Cognitive processes, such as the discovery of relationships between concepts, theoretical premises, and object categories on the basis of specific information provided by textbooks and classroom instruction, require a deep understanding and internalization of cultural knowledge and values. The reason is that both understanding and value internalization determine the process of organizing instruction and learning, as well as the participation of teachers and students during formal instruction.

One of the problems in schooling for some immigrant, refugee and other minority children is that they live a life of hardships. Here are some of the characteristics of this life:

1. Life of poverty and isolation. This means, at best, the lack of privacy in crowded and poorly insulated dwellings, lack of showers and toilet facilities, lack of comfort, and lack of regular medical services. At worst, it means child abuse, malnutrition, poor health and neglect.

2. Cultural and linguistic differences. This entails educational neglect, late exposure to literacy, low school achievement, and often stereotypic classification into learning disability groups.
3. Lack of appreciation for home culture, and lack of self-esteem. This can result in social and economic dependence on low-paying jobs, and low overall achievement aspirations, low income and low social status.

The cultural integration of immigrant and refugee persons takes place after a long period of painful experiences while living in America, and it is characterized by the following features:

1. Late academic intensive socialization, with a better understanding of the functional value of literacy and educational training for survival in America.
2. Genuine discovery and appreciation of mainstream values within their social context, for example, the honor system, the conformity with public rules and regulation in order to act effectively as a group, individual discipline and personal reliability in socially cohesive units, the use of authority and power for the sake of the community, and the need for financial planning.
3. Discovery of racial/ethnic stereotypes in day-to-day interaction with mainstream peers, in reference to the ethnic culture on the part of mainstream persons, and in reference to mainstream culture on the part of minorities.
4. Need for revitalization ceremonies which bring the reaffirmation of one's own traditional cultural values into perspective, in contrast with those more recently acquired in contact with mainstream society.
5. Experimentation in the use of mainstream values to bring desired effects, and partial, gradual, or experimental acceptance.
6. Ability to function in mainstream circles through effective oral and written communication, and to establish personal relationships with members of the mainstream society.
7. Further internalization of selected mainstream values stimulated by expected desirable outcomes such as rewards, access to resources, and recognition of one's own success.
8. Contextualized commitment to abide by mainstream values in specific settings (at work, in public institutions, etc.), and under specific interactional circumstances (dealing with certain kinds of people).

9. Bilingual and bicultural skills to code-switch and use either set of values in different interactional arenas.
10. Skills and long-term commitment to exhibit and promote mainstream values in public settings, provided certain home and community values are protected.

There is a final state of assimilation of immigrant and refugee populations to mainstream society which is often characterized by profound personal changes, including:

1. Keen awareness and priority of social class status, and active membership in middle and upper-middle class organizations.
2. Marriage into a mainstream family equally conscious of social status.
3. Loss of contact with one's own ethnic group and organizations, ethnic peers and ethnic culture.
4. Drastic changes in religious beliefs and practices, from native or ethnic religions to churches of the mainstream population.
5. Increase in educational level and career aspirations and specialization.
6. Decrease in social consciousness about one's ethnic group, and a loss of commitment to serve or assist one's own ethnic peers.
7. Loss of active membership in the extended family, signaled by persistent absence in life cycle crises ceremonies and in other major events previously attended with peer members of ethnic group.

Are American and Hmong cultures incompatible? What is the essence of Hmong culture? How can an American understand mountain people with language and customs totally different and at times incomprehensible to Westerners?

Clearly, educators serving multi-ethnic and multi-lingual communities across the United States must resolve the problem of the cultural gap between themselves and their students. Recent figures (1988) from the Office of Refugee Resettlement indicate that the influx of refugees from all over the world shows no signs of abating soon. As Table 1.2 shows, total refugee admissions for fiscal year 1988 stood at over 75,000.

The problem is not limited to particular areas, and researchers can not say with any certainty what the population projections will be in the future. However, some areas have been more affected than others by the arrival of the thousands of Indochinese coming to the United States. In spite of the

Table 1.2 *Summary of Refugee Admissions to the United States, 1975-1988*

Fiscal Year	Area						TOTAL
	Africa	Asia	Eastern Europe	Soviet Union	Latin America	Near East Asia	
1975	0	135,000	1,947	6,211	3,000	0	146,158
1976	0	15,000	1,756	7,450	3,000	0	27,206
1977	0	7,000	1,755	8,191	3,000	0	19,946
1978	0	20,574	2,245	10,688	3,000	0	36,507
1979	0	76,521	3,393	24,449	7,000	0	111,363
1980	955	163,799	5,025	28,444	6,662	2,331	207,116
1981	2,119	131,139	6,704	13,444	2,017	3,829	159,252
1982	3,326	73,522	10,780	2,756	602	6,369	97,355
1983	2,648	39,408	12,083	1,409	668	5,465	61,681
1984	2,747	51,960	10,285	715	160	5,246	71,113
1985	1,953	49,970	9,350	640	138	5,994	68,045
1986	1,315	45,454	8,713	787	173	5,998	62,440
1987	1,994	40,112	8,606	3,694	315	10,107	64,828
1988	1,588	35,015	7,818	20,421	2,497	8,415	75,754
TOTAL	18,645	884,474	90,460	129,299	32,232	53,654	1,208,764

Source: Report to the Congress: *Refugee Resettlement Program* (1989, Appendix B–14), US Department of State, Bureau for Refugee Programs.

policy of dispersal throughout the United States, secondary migration (as noted previously) brought Hmong, Lao, Vietnamese and Cambodian refugees to unprepared towns and cities all over the country. At latest count, California led the nation in total refugee arrivals (34,860 for 1988), and had 40% of the Indochinese refugee population (Office of Refugee Resettlement, 1989: 21 and Appendix A–15). The same source indicates that, not surprisingly, California now has 33% of refugee children enrolled in schools (1989: Appendix A–21).

Although Indochinese refugees accounted for over 35% of all refugees admitted during 1988 (Office of Refugee Resettlement, 1989: 9) researchers and educators are not faced with a simple challenge of adapting teaching methods to suit one situation in the history of refugee and immigrant arrivals. Rather, they must take the example provided by the arrival of one refugee group — in this instance, primarily the Hmong — and turn solutions into models that can be applied in future situations.

Chapter two

Ethnohistory of the Hmong People

Looking at his mother, Chou, a 5-year-old Hmong child asks her: 'Remember when we were walking in the jungle and crossed a big river?' The mother laughs and shakes her head. 'You were born in America', she says, 'unlike the rest of the family, you are an American.' The child laughs back, not quite convinced, although he knows his mother is telling the truth. Yet, for many Hmong children born in America, the reality of crossing the Mekong River and the experiences in the refugee camps are also their own, because their parents and siblings have talked about them many times.

Oral traditions and recorded personal histories depict the Hmong as a fierce, independent and invincible people who took to the mountains rather than submit to the domination of lowlanders. Their quest for autonomy led them from the forest of southern China to the fertile mountains of Burma, Laos, Vietnam and Thailand. How and why were the Hmong recruited by the armed forces to fight on the side of the Americans against other Indochinese? How is their involvement in the Indochinese wars related to their subsequent resettlement in the West — primarily the United States, but also France, French Guyana, Canada, and Australia?

Traditional and recent subsistence patterns, religious practices, initial and subsequent migrations, and family structure patterns have affected the ways in which Hmong refugees have established themselves in a central west coast California community. Knowledge of Hmong history is particularly critical in view of the psychological and medical complications resulting from their relocation. Whether children were born in Laos, Thailand, or the United States, Hmong history becomes a part of their current common cultural patrimony. Children hear daily about the mountain villages, air strip settlements, and refugee camps from parents and older siblings. There were many relatives left in the villages and camps of Laos and Thailand with whom Hmong refugees maintain strong ties and communicate across continents through letters, cassettes, and telephone.

The Hmong in Laos: Historical Context

Thought to have originated in Mongolia, the Hmong (known in early literature as the *Miao* or *Meo*) settled in the river valleys of northern China 4000 years ago, and eventually moved south, north and west into the highlands where geographical isolation enhanced their linguistic and cultural distinctiveness (Savina, 1930; Graham, 1937; Geddes, 1976; Larteguy, 1979 and Xyooj, 1981).

The name *Miao* has traditionally been applied to many of the related ethnic groups living in south and southwest China. Although the term has become the official label of many groups in China today, it is still considered derogatory by Hmong in China, as well as by those resettled in the United States. The notion of ethnic identity developed by DeVos includes language, religion, cultural traditions, folklore, lifestyle and art. Using similar measurement, Chinese anthropologists distinguish between 70 and 400 different ethnic groups. Southwest China, the home of various Hmong groups, ranges in altitutes from 1000 to 9000 feet. The area is made up of mountain slopes and deep canyons. Writing in an article published in *Haiv Hmoob*, Dr Li Jinchi of the Central Institute of Nationalities, Beijing, notes that as of 1988 there were 5 million Hmong in China. Hmong are distributed throughout the provinces of Guizhou, Hunan, Yunnan, Sichuan, Hubei, Guangxi and Guangtong (Li, 1988: 1).

Persistent questions in Hmong history on the relationship of Chinese Hmong to Hmong living in Laos, Thailand and the United States require research beyond the scope of this book. However, the feeling of kinship between Chinese Hmong and those elsewhere remains strong, as is evidenced by the recent communications (both personal and professional) between Chinese Hmong and Hmong resettled in the United States.

Within the general Hmong group, dialect, dress and general lifestyle define and distinguish subgroups. There are Striped Hmong, Flowery Hmong, White Hmong, and the Blue/Green Hmong — the last two represent groups whose dialects are mutually intelligible, though their pronunciation and vocabulary differ substantially (Heimbach, 1979). There are some linguistic and cultural intra-group differences among the Hmong resulting from their adaptation to the various countries in which they lived, but in spite of these differences they still retain unique common characteristics:

— language with mutually intelligible dialects
— a strong belief in ancestor worship and animism
— a division of labor according to family membership and sex

— a social structure based on kinship ties through patrilineage and clan systems
— a patrivirilocal pattern of residence
— a history of migration from southern China
— a long tradition of being stateless (Lee, 1986: 55).

These are very important cultural distinctive characteristics which identify the social structure of the Hmong and their intricate set of relationships. The pattern of patrilineal clans, groups of males and their families sharing descent from a common male relative and residence with the husband's family, along with the assumed responsibilities by the male-head of the family towards the wife's kin, explains some of the cultural conflicts that surfaced during the relocation of Hmong refugees. They felt morally obliged to protect the family unity along the lines of the patrilineal clans. Out of necessity, some of the social and cultural characteristics of the Hmong noted by Lee such as residence patterns, *swidden* or slash-and-burn agriculture, and other features of their collective activities have been altered, disappeared, or lost significance. Nevertheless, the interdependence of clan members for subsistence, ancestor worship, animism, and the key role of elders (particularly males), continue in the post-resettlement life.

For centuries, the Hmong practiced swidden agriculture by burning virgin forests, letting them lie fallow, and then planting subsistence crops and cash crops. Maintaining a consistent food supply demanded the full participation of all able-bodied family members, who performed the daily tasks of rice cultivation, care of livestock, and vegetable gardening. Hmong men were also involved in hunting and fishing. Swidden cultivation of rice (as opposed to the swamp-rice cultivation practiced by the lowland Lao) rapidly depleted the soil, thus forcing periodic moves. Raising rice and maize as subsistence crops and, later, opium as a cash crop, Hmong families moved approximately every seven to ten years in search of fertile lands (see Geddes, 1976; Cooper, 1979, 1986).

Kinship relationships based on patrilineal clans and patrilineages were essential in cultivation and relocation activities which a single nuclear family could not handle. Kinship ties were critical, both in organizing groups of Hmong and in providing backup resources during relocation. Here, the distinctions between clan, lineage, and nuclear family were very important. A limited number of patrilineal clans (indicated by names now used as surnames — Moua, Xiong, and Vang, for example) formed the basis of traditional Hmong society. Brothers and cousins were all *Kwv Tij*, 'brothers' who mature together creating a cohesive mutually supportive group. A girl, on the other hand, married out into the lineage and clan of her husband. New couples lived in large homes which housed multi-generational households which eventually split into separate dwellings, without losing thier close relationship with the patrilineage.

Clans, composed of localized patrilineages, performed important social, religious and economic functions, often associated with relocation of its patrilineages. The hand labor required for relocation made the clan an essential organizational feature. A wife's relatives — necessarily from a clan other than the husband's — called the *Neej Tsa* (essentially the wife's male siblings' patri-clan) were also an instrumental and supportive group which became handy during relocation.

Religion, too, played an important role in traditional Hmong life. Unlike other ethnic minority groups that incorporated the Buddhist beliefs of the lowland Lao during their residence in Laos, the Hmong (until Christianity was introduced) retained a traditional belief system based on animism and ancestor worship. Living in a world they saw as being populated and controlled by spirits (both of the home and beyond) required vigilant observation of taboos as well as appeasement of spirits and ancestors. Ritual ceremonies were associated with daily and calendrical activities, life-cycle critical events and crises. In times of illness and emergency, a shaman intervened with the spirit world. In trance, the shaman communicated with unseen observers, bringing back from the trance interpretations of the problem and solutions for its resolution.

According to Schein (1986: 73–85), if we look at the linguistic and cultural characteristics of contemporary Hmong living in Laos, Thailand and the United States, and compare them to the Hmong who live in modern south and southwest China, we find significant areas of communality. In contemporary China there are over 1 billion people. Approximately 7%, or 70 million Chinese belong to minority groups called *misu* (nationalities or ethnic groups).

In 1982 there were 4.03 million Miao, representing 7.5% of the entire minority population in China. While the Hmong are presently scattered through the south and southwest, there are some heavier concentrations (54%) in the province of Guizhou. Two of the provinces, Hunan and Yunan, each have 15% of the Hmong population.

The Hmong people are considered semi-nomadic, hill folk, who practice rice and corn agriculture. They are highly diversified and adapted to different ecologies. Many of them are slash-and-burn agriculturists. Some of their groups, such as the Hei (Black Miao), who live in Qingshui, have a sophisticated river economy; they cultivate paddy-rice and other products.

Contemporary Hmong are divided into three major linguistic groups, each with various regional differences and subdialects, but they share about 40% of the vocabulary. The first language is called *Chuan-gian-dian* and used by about 50% of the entire Hmong population; it is spoken in the provinces of Guizhou, Yunan, and Sichuan. The speakers of *Chuan-gian-dian* call themselves Hmoob and are divided into two subgroups, the Hmoob-Dawb (White Hmong) and the Hmoob-Ntsuab (Blue-Hmong), with mutually understandable dialects (Schein, 1986: 79). The second language is *Qian Dong*, also called 'central dialect', and is used by the Hmo or Hmu who live in the province of Guizhow, and constitute about 30% of the Hmong population. The third language is called *Xiang Xi*, also called the 'eastern dialect', and is used by the Qhov Xyooj who live in eastern Hunan and western Guizhow and constitute about 20% of the Hmong population.

There are approximately 200,000 Hmong who speak languages not related to the three groups discussed above. They are speakers of language groups called *Han, Yao* and *Dong*. They are considered Hmong because their culture and ethnic affiliation have been historically linked to the Hmong.

Chinese policy has recently emphasized the development of minority written languages and the use of these languages for education. There are many elementary and secondary schools in which native languages are used for the instruction of minorities. Beijing has pursued liberal policies in support of centers for the development of Institutes for Nationalities — including the Central Institute of Beijing — which function as major centers for the study of ethnic groups (or 'nationalities' as they call them) and to train minority students in math and science.

The Hmong culture in China is characterized by a free and powerful spirit strongly opposed to outside domination and willing to sacrifice everything in order to maintain autonomy. The Hmong people are seen in China as very talented, enjoying diverse forms of artistic expression, music and dancing unique to their people and congruent with their traditional folklore, for example in the context of courtship dances. They use the gong, drums, bamboo pipe organs, and leaf-blowing. They also sing and improvise dialogue.

In Beijing the Central Nationalities Institute celebrates an annual Pan-Miao festival on April 8 in honor of Miao heroes. Part of the underlying policy of Chinese authorities is to favor the concentration of all the Hmong in areas in which their communities can be given the attention and support needed.

From southern China, groups of Hmong moved into Indochina

between 200 and 400 years ago, inhabiting the mountains above 3000 feet. The Hmong shared the higher altitudes with the Iu Mien (formerly known as Yao). The original inhabitants of Laos, the Khmou (formerly known as Kha) had by this time been pushed to the middle altitudes by the lowland Lao, who took control of the river valleys.

The Hmong people refer to Laos as *Peb lub tebchaws* (our country) and as *Lub tebchaws nplog* (the country of the Lao). Indeed Laos has a history of discrimination against minorities (immigrant and indigenous), particularly the mountain people. Yet, Hmong managed eventually to become an integral part of Laos and to participate in its military and economic organizations.

A set of questions have to do with the adaptation of the Hmong to life in Laos and Thailand. What were the stages of cultural adaptation? What changes affected the social organization and the economic life of the Hmong during their years in Laos and Thailand? Smalley (1986: 7–22) outlines the series of stages marking the historical development of the Hmong during their years in Laos, Thailand, and eventually in third country resettlement. As Smalley describes the process, Hmong penetration in Laos was gradual; small numbers of Hmong began to learn to cope with other ethnic groups, especially the Lao and French, but retained a cultural orientation to China and/or North Vietnam. When large numbers of Hmong arrived, they created a strong ethnic community which maintained relative isolation, living in the mountains and avoiding contact with more powerful groups. The relationship between Hmong and other ethnic groups became more stable and Hmong people began to play a significant role in the larger Lao state. Eventually, Hmong were abruptly forced out of their villages into resettlement military villages where they were forced to mingle with other groups and their cultural traditions were curtailed. Following this stage, Hmong people migrated in masses to Thailand and resettled in the United States (Smalley, 1986: 7–8).

Hmong Refugees' Journey to America

Why would the Hmong, who are mountain people living in isolated rural areas, capable of surviving in the most rugged of terrains, and accustomed to privacy and freedom of movement, want to come to a highly industralized country, live in urban areas, often with extreme weather conditions and altogether so different from their place of origin? The answer can be found in the refugee experience precipitated by Hmong involvement with the American military during the Vietnam War. Prior to their arrival in the United States they were displaced by the war and were separated from the extended family, a social unit which performed vital functions in the socialization of children. Unfortunate and unexpected turns of events took them over long distances, to live in refugee camps, to find ingenious ways of qualifying for refugee status and residence in the United States, and finally to arrive and relocate in a new country under traumatic circumstances.

While many of the adult Hmong refugees are illiterate in any language, some can read in English, French or Lao, as they come from the French Indochinese region of Southeast Asia and are exposed to these three languages. Text has not been the main instrument for the transmission of their cultural values, because Hmong have relied on a rich oral cultural tradition for many decades. Text, however, became crucial during the period of transition from Indochina to America. The consequences of understanding and keeping documents, of having in writing the family name, place of origin, age of members, and other relevant information became a matter of life and death.

Hmong people are currently living in China, Thailand, Vietnam, Laos and in Western resettlement areas, primarily the United States and Canada. The Hmong are traditionally organized in peasant communities using slash-and-burn agriculture. They see themselves as members of a single sociocultural unit, as one people, regardless of dialectic and subcultural differences resulting from years of separation, migration and geographical distances. A history of colonial exploitation, of labor force distribution along the lines of ethnic membership, of racial tensions, lack of technical sophistication — especially on the part of the hill tribes Hmong — and of isolation of various Hmong groups, has placed the Hmong people at the bottom of Indochina's social stratification. Such status was reflected in the treatment received by the various Indochinese refugee groups both in the resettlement camps and in the United States.

In the relatively short time between the mid-1940s and the late 1970s, the Hmong lifestyle, cultural traditions, economy and religion changed dramatically. The Indochinese wars ended their isolation and put them in contact with other Indochinese peoples. Their subsistence activities expanded, their sophistication in dealing socially and in business activities with other cultural groups increased.

By the mid-1970s the total Hmong population exceeded 3.5 million. Approximately 3 million Hmong were estimated to live in China; 300,000 in the Northern Provinces of Laos, 220,000 in Vietnam; and 50,000 in Thailand (Yang Dao, 1975: 28). The Indochinese wars had converted the Hmong into refugees, beginning in the 1940s. Some became quasi-nomadic fighters, and others were subsequently trained by the CIA to become the secret guerrillas. When the Americans abandoned Indochina in 1975, many Hmong, fearing for their lives under the Communist regime, crossed the Mekong River and escaped to Thailand, where they regrouped in refugee camps. Refugees in Thailand went through quite an ordeal, sometimes for years, before they were accepted by resettlement agencies as potential candidates to emigrate to the United States or to other Western countries. It is important to keep in mind that the Hmong are a monolithic group; through historical events their lives as refugees (affected in diverse ways by the host country and their personal experiences) have been perceived as similar, and have often placed them in a single category of Indochinese refugees regardless of cultural and historical differences. The La Playa Hmong families came primarily from three provinces in Laos, Xieng Khouang (a central area which was hardest hit by the war), Nam Tha (northwest), and Sam Neua (northeast). They have different backgrounds, educational levels and experiences. Some Hmong remained very isolated, even during the war years. It is important to be sensitive to Hmong people's differences within their own group, as well as in contrast with other Indochinese groups.

The lives of Hmong refugees revolved around their war experiences. Kirton describes some of these experiences as follows:

> The men, some of whom were conscripted at the age of 12 or 13, were rarely seen during the periods of heavy fighting; they returned home only for short visits or to recuperate. The women and children continued to tend the fields, the gardens, and the animals. The death of a child, marriages, births, and bombings identified the passing months and years. Normal events — a husband's flirting with a potential second wife, an illness requiring medical treatment in Vietnam, sending a son away to school — were interrupted by periods spent hiding in the jungle or fleeing communist troops... One women told us of a day early in her marriage when a plane arrived to take a group of wives to visit their husbands stationed in a village in northern Laos. Arriving at the camp, the woman was annoyed when friends told her that her husband was seeing a young girl; they said he intended to marry her. Annoyance turned to fury when her husband suggested she might like to give the shoes she was wearing to the girl. Retelling the story years later, the woman laughingly told us the girls in the areas had been so beautiful that the soldiers were reluctant to leave (Kirton, 1985: 58).

The dominant themes and stories narrated by Hmong people reflect vivid memories of their escape from Laos and their experiences in the refugee camps. Pre-arrival experiences help explain Hmong adjustment to American society and their lifestyle in La Playa. At times, the psychological disorders related to post-traumatic stress were severe and painful.

Recent Rapid Sociocultural Changes

Until relatively recently, Hmong universally shared the fundamental elements of Hmong culture (Lee, 1982). The establishment of a French protectorate in 1887 within what is now Laos irrevocably altered the traditional isolation of the Hmong and established permanent economic and political institutions which determined the patterns of interaction between the ethnic Lao and the minority groups. French rule filtered from the capital to villages through Vietnamese and Lao administrators. The development of Laos under the French was minimal and the impact of the French regime on education (see Bliatout, Downing, Lewis and Yang, 1988, for descriptions) was limited to the ethnic Lao. Thus the oppression experienced by minority groups, the Hmong, Iu Mien, Khmou, and others was intensified during the French colonial occupation of Laos, in spite of the fact that these minorities paid as many taxes to the government (in the form of goods and services) as the ethnic Lao.

During this period of colonial inequity individual Hmong leaders started to take their first steps towards participation in national politics, by organizing revolts against local heads of government. These activities geared to end the oppressive conditions imposed by the French led to the appointment of the first Hmong to local administrative posts of Hmong settlements. Competition for these posts by members of various Hmong clans resulted in eventual splintering of Hmong loyalties during the World War II and beyond. During the Japanese invasion of Indochina, clan leaders aligned themselves with either the French colonialists or the Japanese troops. The split continued during the post-World War II struggle for independence. Some Hmong supported the French, while others sided with future members of the communist pathet Lao (Lee, 1982).

American interests in Laos and Vietnam grew during the decades of civil war and political instability in Indochina. The involvement of the CIA eventually led to the establishment of the famous Armee Clandestine under the command of a Hmong military leader, General Van Pao, who was the Royal Lao Army Commander of the Second Military Region. Van Pao recruited the Hmong into what came to be equated with the secret guerrilla forces. The Hmong lost more lives in the civil war than any other ethnic group in Laos, and many other Hmong had to escape. About 30,000 Hmong people were killed and several hundred thousand were displaced (Lee, 1982). The Hmong recruited for the Armee Clandestine were supported by the CIA, who planted the seeds for the eventual resettlement of the Hmong in the United States. The *Hmong Resettlement Study*, issued by the Office of Refugee Resettlement (1989), quotes versions of 'The Promise' that U.S. officials made to the Hmong. Photographs of officials and testimonies collected from resettled refugees demonstrate that the Hmong believed this promise and felt they would be compensated and protected in the event of military defeat by the Communists.

Diversification within the Hmong

Some studies portray the Hmong as a homogeneous group of rural Indochinese mountaintop dwellers who (Lemoine, 1972; Geddes, 1976) transferred directly from the mountains to San Diego, Santa Ana or Minneapolis. The reality of the war and resettlement camp experiences diversified Hmong people significantly. For those involved directly in the guerrilla war, life had changed drastically through brutal experiences, training and contact with Americans. As can be expected, some Hmong villages remained undisturbed during the war, but they were the exception.

For many Hmong families the two decades after World War II brought a new market economy, Christian missionaries who actively proselytized, Western doctors and medicines, new subsistence patterns (USAID food drops, as well as wet-rice cultivation), and life in internal refugee camps. Garret (1974) and Yang (1975) have documented these changes. They claim that the fourteen years of war resulted in more economic progress than the previous fifty years of peace.

After two decades of internecine warfare, the fall of the last coalition government (the Provisional Government of National Union) in May 1975 ended one phase of the hostilities. With the flight of General Vang Pao to safety in Thailand, thousands of Hmong were left behind unprotected, thus beginning another sad episode in the history of Hmong migrations. What happened to these families left behind, and how did they manage to be sent to America, and specifically to La Playa, California? The following attempts to summarize individual experiences which illustrate vividly this part of Hmong history.

Ethnic boundaries, which once drove the Hmong into highland isolation, were after the war no longer socially or geographically significant, nor coterminous with environmental boundaries. Hmong men fought alongside Lao, Iu Mien, and Khmou soldiers. This did not, by any means, eliminate ethnic boundaries and tension between the various groups, but it led to some intermarriage, exchange of languages, and cooperation during the war effort. Hurried internal refugee migrations following General Van Pao's flight brought about intermingling and further cooperation of the various ethnic groups.

Sociocultural Changes and Their Effect on Kinship

The war had made subsistence farming largely impossible; consequently, many depended for their survival on government food drops. The repercussions of both the food drops and the hiring of soldiers reached far beyond the Hmong home. Military employment, access to markets, and increased demand for imported goods opened up new subsistence opportunities for Indochinese. Individual entrepreneurs, who saw avenues for economic upward mobility in small import and sale business, found independent action more appropriate and feasible, particularly in the face of disagreements within the lineage group.

Kao, now a 45-year-old man of La Playa, was the oldest son. He left his parents' home to join the army at Long Cheng, Laos. Contrary to traditional practice, he chose his own wife against his parents' will. When Kao married the girl of his choice, peaceful coexistence in the household was impossible. All these actions put some distance between him and his brothers, and Kao and his new bride moved to the military settlement at Long Cheng. Although Kao and his wife visited his family frequently, they never shared a household again — until they arrived in La Playa.

Life was not easy for women, and it changed significantly as well during the pre-resettlement years. Most of them saw their husbands only during their infrequent leaves, and continued traditional pursuits of vegetable gardening and raising a few domestic animals. Others, however, began small marketing ventures, selling goods in the city market place, or purchasing products for resale in the village.

A woman, now in her early 40s, laughed reminiscing about her fear at joining her new household after marriage. She did not sleep, eat, or talk for several days. Soon after the wedding ceremony her husband returned to his military unit, leaving her with his clan, virtual strangers. By the time he returned on his next leave, she had grown quite used to his family. When she again saw her husband, he seemed like a stranger. Her life had taken on a certain rhythm that included cooking, caring for her new baby, and helping with the work of the household. Her best friend (another newly married young girl) helped her to adjust; they often spent the night together. Except for the arrival of her baby, she had essentially returned to single status (albeit socially restricted).

The tragedies and opportunities of the war years changed the traditional kinship structure by forcing reliance on a wider group of relatives (on both husband's and wife's sides) and friends. As the intensity of the fighting increased, the need for relocation became urgent, as did the need for a support group of relatives. Depending on the resources of the in-laws, a man and his family might temporarily or permanently move in with (or move closer to) his wife's brothers or his sister's husband. In times of emergency, it was worthwhile to maintain the highest possible number of support relationships. In this way, for example, Neng, with his parents and male cousins unavailable to him, joined the household of his sister. In another case, an orphaned man and his younger brother lived with his wife's parents.

Initially established to serve the ethnic Lao, the schools gradually opened their doors to more and more Hmong children. Access to education introduced a major factor changing the lives of some Hmong families. Only those who had money, and either lived close to a school or had relatives in town, could send a child to school. Typically, a family had only enough money to support one child in school; and the other children contributed to the family's labor force. Thus, the experience of education separated not only Hmong families, but also Hmong siblings within the same family.

A young college student described his school experience in Laos:

> I have never lived with my family until this year. I am so used to independence, that it is hard for me to adjust now. I left home when I was about six or seven years old. My mother was already dead when my father sent me to school. They took me and my cousin to the city. We lived with a family of relatives (Kirton, 1987).

This student's aunt remembers packing food and clothing to last several weeks, loading the horses and walking the two children to town. From the time the boys started school, they never again took part in the family subsistence activities that kept their siblings busy. Occasionally girls also went to school. A woman in her early 30s told us that when she was a girl she was determined to go to school. Her father objected, so she slipped away from her responsibilities each morning to follow her brother to a school close to their village in northwestern Laos. Her younger sister, who was left with additional chores, was not amused.

There were three brothers in a family. The parents sent the oldest brother, Pao, to school. He went on to become a respected Christian pastor, literate in Lao and in Hmong. The second brother, Lue, took his older brother's responsibilities; as his parents aged, Lue became the head of a large extended family, responsible for feeding and clothing his parents, his own family, and his younger siblings. He alternated between farming and soldiering, but never attended school in Laos. The third brother, Tou, was attending school in Laos when the entire family decided to leave for Thailand.

One of the most drastic sociocultural changes was the conversion of many Hmong people to Christianity. Religion was the very foundation of their social, political and economic life. As is usually the case with conversions of indigenous peoples to Christianity, there was a wide range of acceptance of particular aspects of the new religion. Because the Hmong had contact with different religious groups, Catholics, Seventh Day Adventists, Jehovah's Witnesses, and the Christian and Missionary Alliance, their Christian belief system is highly diversified and has impacted differentially on family home life.

Two older women, related through marriage to two brothers, sat at home in La Playa working on their *paj ntaub* (traditional Hmong embroidery) and described, first with indifference and then vividly, the events associated with the village's change of religion. The missionaries' arrival and early work were taken up in a series of meetings with the elders that culminated in a final shamanistic event, in which local shamans performed their duties for the last time, set fire to their drums and other paraphernalia, and threw them over the side of the mountain. The elders proposed that the village accept the teaching of the missionaries.

Another old woman, herself a shaman when younger, explained why she gave enough credence to the French and American priests to abandon both her practice of shamanistic curing and the performance of traditional rituals at home:

The priest told me none of my children would die if I did what he told me. I had four children, and three others that had died. When the priest came, all four of my remaining children were sick. He told me they would not die, so I gave everything up to him. It worked, too; none of those children died. *THEY* went away crying, and the priest took care of everything.

When asked: 'Who went away crying?' She replied:

The spirits. The spirits went away crying. I saw them. I talked to them, and I told them they had to go away. I told them the priest was there, and that he would hit them. I told them to go away and not come back anymore, so they did. After that the children did not die. The only people who died were the old people who got to the time in their lives to die. Some children died after that too, but they were just the ones whose spirits did not want to stay with their parents (Kirton, 1987).

Conversion to Christianity, as it was expected, divided families as individual members either fully accepted the new religion, or resisted it. A couple converted when their son threatened them with a wife. A girl's family consented to her marriage on the condition that the entire household accept Christianity. Families frequently took one step toward Christianity and two steps back. Some Hmong individuals whose families had converted returned to the traditional religion upon marrying someone who had not 'abandoned the spirits' (*Lawb dab*).

Conversion to Christianity or observance of traditional animistic ritual resulted in various non-conventional, non-clan-structured alliances of individuals, who were searching for support in their religious practices. For example, in a patri-clan composed of five brothers, four converted to Christianity and one decided to move out to live with his in-laws, who had retained traditional religious beliefs. In another family, there were two sisters, Mao, the older, and Choua, the younger. Mao and her husband moved ahead of the fighting in Sayaboury province for years, eventually joining the hundreds of refugees being supported by USAID food drops. While still in Laos they converted to Christianity and — in their mid-50s — learned to read and write Hmong in the Thai camps. They left Laos in 1975 and were among the first families to arrive in La Playa. Because of their involvement in the church and their literacy in Hmong, they became pivotal members of the community.

Choua and her husband, on the other hand, succeeded in staying away from active fighting for much longer. They did not join the flock of internal refugees, but did leave Laos after 1975. Neither Christianity nor literacy changed their traditional orientation. It was not until resettlement became imminent that, under pressure from Mao and her husand, Choua gave up her active shamanistic practice.

The changes in Hmong tradition and lifestyle during the Indochinese wars, particularly those associated with changes in religion, provide the central themes of recent novels written by Nyiajpov Lis (Pao Lee), a Hmong resettled in Australia. Lis's books, written in White Hmong, are entitled, *Lub Neej Daitaw* (1986a), *Vim Leejtwg* (1986b), and *Txojsaw Lhub* (1987). In his novels, lovers can not marry because the boy is not Christian and the girl's family refuses to give consent, or lovers can not marry because the boy must first finish school. In one of the novels, a boy who has pursued his lover and accepted the condition to finish school, goes on to graduate, but finds out that in the meantime another man has made a favorable offer to the girl's parents. The student is left crying. In another, lovers can not marry because the boy goes off to war. Visiting in the city, a boy begins flirting with a Hmong girl who works in the local market selling produce. He promises eternal love to her, however, the distance and hardships of war lead him eventually to betray his love for her. In Lis' novels traditional values of loyalty, family unity, and obedience to elders are exhibited in a new cultural context that includes Christianity, civil war, education, and entrepreneurship.

Chapter three

The Hmong at La Playa

A steady stream of Hmong refugees began to pour into La Playa and other towns across the United States in 1975. The stream continued, sometimes rising and sometimes abating, over the next decade. Emerging from their nightmare of bombing, ambushes, 'yellow rain', and starvation, the Hmong faced a new challenge — adjustment to life in a new country. The process of adjustment was formed by 1) the special circumstances of the Hmong arrival, 2) the goals of American officials, and 3) the Hmong reaction to resettlement. Working with this new population presented unforeseen problems, as refugees, motivated by rational considerations of self-preservation, rather than complacency with the circumstances, made choices that did not fit the plan of the government officials.

After the initial support, involvement on the part of the host community dwindled, leaving the Hmong self-reliant by necessity. While Hmong were successful in finding employment after the establishment of their community, deeper problems persisted — particularly evident in the dearth of effective communication between the Hmong and their American hosts.

Hmong Arrive at La Playa

In contrast with other groups of refugees that arrived in the United States, the Hmong came under particularly difficult circumstances. First, the culture and way of life of the Hmong differed dramatically from that of any other refugees previously known in the United States. Chapter 2 dealt with the individual differences in experience that diversified the Hmong people. In spite of this diversity, however, the Hmong had in common the lack of contact with Western societies, and as a group they knew little about what to expect from life in the United States. Before their arrival, only a few Hmong had had any experience coping with everyday matters of urban life — wage labor, banks, schools, hospitals, police, and the welfare department; few had sufficient command of the English language for communication in those institutions. Additionally, there was no established Hmong community in the United States to ease refugees' anxiety of adjustment and to assist them. Hmong refugees were virtually the first Hmong people to settle in the United States, thus they lacked the resources and expertise of a receiving ethnic group.

Most importantly, the Hmong brought with them the special needs of a refugee population, different from those of immigrant populations. Immigrants and refugees alike must cope with the new cultural environment and unexpected lifestyle of the host community, its customs, language, and traditions. However, the circumstances that force refugees to uproot themselves make their experience a fundamentally different and unique one. Immigrants voluntarily leave their home countries in search of economic opportunities. Refugees are forced to flee in order to keep their life and freedom. They seek refuge as the only chance for physical survival; the more sudden the departure is, the more psychologically damaging the experience becomes (Kunz. 1973).

The desperate effort to survive, first during the war and later during the escape and the journey to resettlement camps, is an experience that gives refugees a feeling of invulnerability (Keller, 1975). However, refugees also leave with a burden of guilt — for having left too early, too late, or merely for surviving when so many others did not. Refugee experiences following flight — particularly given the crowding and inactivity associated with life in the camps — also take their toll and leave permanent scars. Observers of the camp experiences during the early waves of refugees between 1975 and 1981 (Kelly, 1977; Liu *et al.*, 1979; Justus, 1976) have noted refugees' feelings of isolation, resentment, and dependency similar to those of the World War II refugees (Murphy, 1955).

Refugees also left Laos and Thailand with a legacy of physical problems, some of which only showed up after years in the United States. Health officials screening new arrivals had a relatively narrow and straightforward mission: diagnosing and treating the high incidence of tuberculosis, hepatitis, parasites, malaria, and syphilis (Muecke, 1983:836). More difficult health problems had to be faced later, when refugees complained of chronic ailments. Some problems resulted from malnutrition and recurring infections. High blood pressure, diabetes, kidney and gallstones, kidney damage, liver damage, and hearing problems (ailments that are frequent in an elder population) also occurred. Yet another health problem peculiar to refugee populations was the emergence of post-traumatic stress disorder. For example, fear, guilt, and sorrow which had been repressed during the years of war and dislocation, were translated into a variety of physical symptoms not easily identified (Muecke, 1983: 836 Kirton, 1985: 99–103).

Resettlement Program

With the decision for the emergency resettlement of thousands of Indochinese refugees to the United States, government officials and voluntary agencies began planning for their arrival. Three goals figured predominantly in their efforts — dispersal, disease control and economic self-sufficiency.

Goals of American Officials

The primary goal was to disperse the refugee population through various locations in order to avoid overloading any particular area and draining its resources. By scattering the refugees rather than clustering them in targeted areas, so the planners reasoned, one would also minimize potential conflicts with members of the host communities.

The second important concern was to diagnose and treat the acute diseases mentioned above. By establishing rigorous medical screening and treatment, health officials hoped to prevent diseases prevalent among the Indochinese population (such as tuberculosis and hepatitis) from spreading to the general population of the host communities.

The third important concern of the government officials was to arrange for private sponsorship and immediate job placement, in order to prevent long-term welfare dependency and help refugees quickly become economically self-sufficient. For those refugees unable to obtain jobs immediately, local agencies established vocational training programs and English-as-a-Second-Language instruction.

Despite the planning that went into the resettlement of the Indochinese refugees, the task of dealing with such a large and diverse population proved to be more formidable than officials had anticipated. A serious problem emerged from the very structure of the resettlement program, producing unexpected responses on the part of refugees. The refugee response, or 'secondary migration' (moving from the site of initial resettlement), surprised and frustrated resettlement planners and workers.

Rather than instituting a single resettlement plan coordinated by a central American authority, the major responsibility for the Indochinese resettlement program was left in the hands of a wide range of voluntary agencies, operating with good intentions, but with diverse, and at times, inconsistent policies. Voluntary agencies were plagued by conflicts in policy and lack of experience in personnel clearly unprepared for working with Hmong refugees.

This phenomenon is also mentioned in accounts of how earlier refugee populations had been handled. Eisenstadt noted the importance of standardized procedures, expectations, treatment, and provisions in resettlement programs (1954: 173). This is perhaps even more important in the case of the Indochinese refugees who had come to this country expecting the U.S. government to fulfill its promise in return for their services during the war.

As the resettlement process unfolded, however, different policy interpretation among voluntary agencies ranged from discrepancies in the use of per capita allotments for refugee families, to overt disagreement on the particular ways of helping refugees best achieve economic self-sufficiency. The solutions involved long-term, full-time English language training programs, or immediate employment in a low-paying job. Evaluators of refugee programs frequently criticized the lack of uniformity in resettlement goals and in program implementation, noting that program inconsistencies increased resentment and competition among the refugees (Liu *et al.*, 1979: 164–173; Gim and Litwin, 1980: 19–27; Plant, 179: 55; Scott, 1979: 78–85).

In brief, finding themselves scattered around this country, recipients of varying types and degrees of services and support, the Hmong responded by moving from their initial resettlement sites. Refugees compared services, benefits and living conditions, and worked toward reunification. When refugees sponsored in Iowa, Rhode Island, or Minnesota pooled their resources to join their families in San Diego, Santa Ana, or La Playa, it became clear that the planners had been short-sighted.

Thus the initial arrival of refugees was but the first chapter in the resettlement process. The pattern of the initial resettlement and subsequent secondary migrations brought the refugee dilemma to towns and cities across the United States at different times and under different conditions (McInnes, 1981; Thao, 1982; Montero, 1979; Haines, 1982). Refugees arriving in areas of high concentration such as Minneapolis or San Diego early in the resettlement process found highly developed refugee services, whereas those riding the wave of secondary migration into Fresno, Sacramento, and Merced in California's central valley discovered county systems overwhelmed and unprepared for the number of new residents.

Creation of La Playa Hmong Community

From a few original familes in 1976, La Playa grew to 426 Hmong people in 1985. La Playa provides an immediate and vivid example of the process of refugee resettlement and adjustment taking place across the United States. The next section charts the development of the Hmong community in La Playa. Although each resettlement community has its own character and personality, the discussion that follows outlines the pressures and challenges faced by Hmong families in any host community.

Initial Resettlement in La Playa

The first Hmong to arrive in La Playa belonged to one extended family which grew into a community as individual members of this family either sponsored or attracted, through secondary migration, their siblings, in-laws, cousins, and other relatives. Since many community members are connected through birth, marriage, and friendship, the community seems tightly-knit. However, important divisions within the community also exist.

Observing the La Playa Hmong, one notices traditional alliances based on geographical origin, clan, lineage, and dialect which serve both to unite and divide the community. The way the Hmong people have been thrown together in resettlement in the United States created new relationships within the Hmong community that cut across and modified traditional alliances.

Before the disruption of the war, groups of Hmong people were separated geographically, producing cultural, experiential, and linguistic idiosyncrasies. Speakers of the two major dialects tended to form separate villages. Thus, for example, White Hmong members of the Yang clan in Xieng Khouang province might have little in common with Blue/Green Yang living in the northwest, except that they belonged to the same clan. Division and behavioral differences between the White and Blue/Green Hmong people have persisted during the resettlement process, but they have been able to transcend these differences, invoking clan alliances in the interest of mutual support and economic survival. On the other hand, there are situations in which other factors (such as differences in religious belief) put clan members in opposition to each other. Understanding the process of Hmong resettlement requires identifying the sources of community unity and divisiveness; both play an important role in the life of the community.

On the basis of geographical origin, La Playa residents divide into two basic groups, one much larger than the other. Group I includes both White and Blue/Green Hmong people, there is a prevailing feeling of unity created by marriage ties and shared military experience.

Originally, one extended family consisting of parents, several of their children, and their children's families (the family of one son and of several daughters) arrived in La Playa through the sponsorship of a local church. The community expanded as this family sponsored additional relatives. Others arrived in waves of secondary or even tertiary migrations as Hmong refugees successfully reunited their extended families; siblings, in-laws, widows, and orphans were brought into La Playa community.

The community regards the members of this extended family and their relatives as founders of the La Playa Hmong community. Several men from these original lineages continue to play pivotal spiritual, religious, political and liaison roles in the Hmong and mainstream communities. The head of the first family resettled is the most respected elder in the community and intervenes in family disputes and community problems. He is also the leader of one of the two major church groups, and as such he is visible and active at community gatherings, weddings, New Year celebrations, and parties. He leads the community in prayer, gives instructions on proper behaviour, and often takes the opportunity to tell folktales (*dab neeg*).

The elected representatives to the Lao Family Community (the nation-wide Hmong mutual-aid association founded by General Vang Pao) as well as the elected leaders of La Playa Hmong community, are usually chosen from the founding lineages. For example, the leader of one of these lineages, who commands respect because of his past military leadership, was a natural choice for the position of local Hmong leader or 'gatekeeper' (as they have translated the title of the local leader). The responsibilities of the 'gatekeeper' include not only supervising the activities of the community, but also communicating with representatives of other Hmong settlements.

Community elders hold positions of spiritual, religious and political leadership in their lineage, while the young and educated men of those same lineages act as liaisons with Americans. Of the local Hmong refugees, these young men came to the United States already fluent in English and with some skills. They provide an illustration of the critical role that individuals' pre-resettlement experience and English language skills have in economic adjustment. Because of their relatively high educational level, past employment with the American government, or close association with General Vang Pao, they had top resettlement priority. Further, as early arrivals, these men had access to resettlement jobs while they lasted, thereby establishing themselves as authorities on Hmong culture for the Americans and on American culture for the Hmong.

Except for one extended family from eastern Laos, all other families in La Playa (forming Group II) came from the northwest.

Local Response to Hmong Families

The initial response from the host society to the arrival of the Indochinese refugees came from the elementary school, the adult English classes, the sponsoring churches, and eventually the resettlement agency. Developing programs appropriate for the refugees was particularly difficult for the elementary school and the adult school; before 1975 the non-English-speaking residents of La Playa had been either Spanish-speaking immigrants from Mexico and Central America or foreign families connected with the university. The school response to the arrival of refugee students will be discussed in greater depth in the following chapters.

Teachers chosen on the basis of flexible and innovative methods began the adult language program. The program grew as the refugee community grew; at its peak, the program included all-day English and vocational training, as well as evening English classes. The dedication and long-term commitment of teachers played an important part in the day-to-day resettlement experience. For many refugees, friendships with teachers provided the only contact with Americans.

Although sponsoring churches handled the initial resettlement of the refugees in La Playa, responsibility shifted to the resettlement agency, the Indochinese Project (ICP), in 1977. Funded through the Department of Health, Education, and Welfare — now the Department of Health and Human Services — the ICP received funds for a wide range of refugee services — school registration, outreach, social adjustment, transportation, housing, vocational counselling, and health screening.

Activities of the Hmong Community

Many Americans who deal on a superficial level with the Hmong refugees are either unaware of the developments within the community itself or they do not acknowledge them. Resettlement is too often seen as a process in which the host society serves, trains and molds newly-arrived refugees into productive members of the large community. The reality is that the Hmong themselves in La Playa and other communities have, out of necessity, become responsible for their own resettlement.

Hmong community programs, ranging from mutual economic or

social support to entertainment, supplemented the resettlement efforts of the ICP in the host society. An example is the Lao Family Community organization mentioned earlier, which consists of clan-based associations and informal networks of Hmong family members and friends, and provides mutual support among the refugees. Under the direction of General Vang Pao, the Lao Family Community links Hmong families all over the United States and facilitates ongoing communication.

In larger communities, the Lao Family Community organization is very actively providing English classes, vocational training, and interpreter services. In La Playa, however, it serves more as an emergency resource that can be tapped through local connections. Additional mutual support comes from local clan organizations, which in this case override differences in geographical origin and dialect. Clan members share housing, contribute to festivities hosted by the clan, and lend money to each other.

On a more informal level, mutual economic and moral support between relatives and friends has played a major role in successful resettlement — particularly in the case of those Hmong people who have invested their life-savings in the purchase of their own homes. Reciprocal financial support enabled some extended families to buy homes, thus establishing themselves permanently in the area.

Among the refugee community projects, local Americans have probably been least aware of the educational programs. Although several Indochinese community members would like to establish continuing classes both in Hmong and Lao, they have not yet been able to do so because qualified instructors do not have time. Two teachers organized classes in Hmong literacy, one specifically for older community members and primarily attended by women, and the other for all ages. These classes were very popular but did not last long.

The New York celebrations and soccer league activities are the most visible community events. Although the impact of the New Year, which falls in November or December, is sometimes dampened by the weather and the popularity of larger gatherings in other communities, the local celebration continues to be an important part of community life. On-going activities of the soccer league provide the most constant source of entertainment. Teams play in all of the California refugee communities, often in coordination with weddings and other gatherings.

Another community activity that significantly affects resettlement is church involvement. For many Hmong in La Playa church participation takes precedence over everything except family and job. Although church membership is beginning to diversify, community religious activities during most of the resettlement period centered around two major

Christian groups. The initial Hmong refugees, as well as many of those who followed them to La Playa, considered themselves Christian many years before resettlement. The religious head of the smaller group is the patriarch of the founding family of the community. He presides over Bible study and prayer meetings held twice a week in his home. At his request, the children attend Sunday school at the local Methodist Church.

The other religious group is associated with the Christian and Missionary Alliance (CAMA), whose missionaries have long been active in Laos and in refugee camps. This is now the larger of the two groups, and is highly organized, both locally and in conjunction with other CAMA groups all over the United States. Hmong church members organize weekly prayer meetings, a church service on Sunday, and religious instruction for the children. American church pastors have Bible study for the children and occasionally deliver the sermon through an interpreter. In addition to these weekly activities, members also participate in special groups for men, women, and teenagers; church activities dominate the leisure time of many La Playa Hmong families.

Several families (all from northwestern Laos) continue to identify with the churches to which they converted while living in Laos, such as the Catholic Church and the Seventh Day Adventist, and still attend services held by those churches locally. For Christian Hmong, church choice depends primarily on personal preference and family ties, for they see only minimal differences between the church groups. As the Hmong explain these differences, the Seventh Day Adventists do not eat pork, the CAMA try not to work on Sundays, and one group worships only at home. A church offering special activities (a Christian program, for example) may attract the entire Hmong community. Denominational affiliation is less important than the distinction between Christian and non-Christian.

Not all Hmong have converted to Christianity. A few La Playa families do not identify themselves as Christian, and even church-goers vary in motivation and the extent to which they reject traditional beliefs. Some Hmong people have joined Christian churches in the sincere belief that Christianity represents the one road to salvation, while others say they attend church to conform to 'American' behavior. Dedicated church-goers who want to become as American as possible may still resort to consulting a shaman, practice occasional spirit worship, and fear the return of troublesome spirits.

In spite of differences in religious beliefs, the La Playa Hmong see themselves as basically a Christian community, and they cite this as important for their adjustment. The majority of the community members point positively to the absence of regular spirit worship, ancestor worship, and shaman sessions. No paraphernalia for traditional religious practices are visible in La Playa community, as they are in Fresno, Santa Ana, or Minneapolis.

The La Playa Hmong Community in 1985

At the time of our research, the community consisted of eleven clans, with ninety families. In this context, 'family' refers to units consisting of a married couple, a married couple and children, or a parent and children. Households, then, are made up of one or more (usually three to four) families. Twenty individuals — widows, unmarried siblings, orphans, and single men who came to La Playa to work — live with extended families. Fifty-seven families (62% of the population) are Blue/Green Hmong, and thirty-three (or 38%) are White Hmong. Most people under the age of 65 (about 76%) found employment. Seventeen of the families (25% of the population) receive Aid to Families with Dependent Children (Kirton, 1985:85).

During our research, the local Hmong population totalled 426 and appeared stable (except for growth through births). Throughout most of the resettlement period, the community was residentially concentrated, which undoubtedly improved resettlement conditions for those at home during the day and fostered the development of informal help networks. Recent movement out of the immediate La Playa area spread the population over a wider geographical area and diversified what had been fairly uniform living conditions (Kirton, 1985:86).

The La Playa ambiance differs markedly from that of surrounding areas; it is a small and compact community, consisting largely of rental apartment buildings constructed with university students in mind. Most Hmong live in minimally maintained apartments with Spartan furnishings. Hmong buying houses usually move outside La Playa into lower-middle to middle class neighborhoods of single family dwellings. Although the homes they purchase may be as sparsely furnished as those in La Playa, they are spacious and in much better condition.

Inward and outward migration constantly affects the community's composition, but the stability of the founding families provides continuity. Most of those who leave go to California's central valley towns — Fresno, Visalia, Tulare, Merced, Stockton, and Sacramento. Others move to a neighboring town where rents are lower, but they can still commute to work. Reasons for the moves in and out of the La Playa community vary. Those moving in joined relatives in La Playa or came because of employment opportunities, but this is controlled by the cost and availability of housing. Only a few local landlords accept large extended families or households, and Hmong move to La Playa only when affordable housing is vacated by other Hmong families. Movement between La Playa area and neighboring towns is frequent, and many families have gone repeatedly from one to the other and back again.

Recently, the increase in the cost of housing in La Playa is given as the main reason Hmong move away. In comparison to other areas, La Playa, which is adjacent to the university, has the least expensive housing and the largest concentration of rental apartments. It is often the only option for many students, refugees, low-income families, and undocumented workers. Yet, Hmong people find it too costly and keep moving north in search of less expensive apartments.

The scarcity and high cost of housing force residential combinations varying from the traditional pattern. Researchers disagree on the rigidity of the traditional pattern of Hmong patrilocal or patrivirilocal residence — that which is located near the male members of the clan (as used by Cooper, 1979: 178; Geddes, 1976: 22; Bernatzik, 1970: 43; Lemoine, 1972: 139). La Playa Hmong refer to this as the preferred pattern, but vary in their adherence to it. Even when patrilocal residence is possible, families sometimes choose to live with the wife's relatives. Other combinations new since resettlement include unrelated nuclear families of a single clan and combined White Hmong/Blue Hmong households.

Employment has been an important factor in shaping the La Playa community. Residents are very proud of their high employment, compared to communities such as Fresno and Merced. The employment of one of the early arrivals in a local electronics factory led to a steady source of jobs for almost everyone in the community who wanted to work. Although wages are lower at this company than at other local factories, the company has provided employment to workers with no English and no marketable skills. At one point, most of the employed Hmong of La Playa worked at this single factory, but since then they have branched out to other companies offering more money.

Of the 426 Hmong residents in 1985, 172 could be considered 'employable'. Included in this category are all adults over 18, not in high school, and not yet eligible for Supplemental Security Income (SSI) on the basis of age or disability. Circumstances such as child care problems, lack of aptitude, and physical ailments prevent some people from working. Others in the 'employable' group attend the local community college full time. Still others with large families do not work, because it is not financially practical for them to give up welfare payments for minimum wage.

However, they are included in the general category 'employable', because others in the same situations work. The discussion is further complicated by the exclusion from this category of high school students who may, in fact, be working part time; their inclusion would distort the picture (Kirton, 1985: 89–90).

Of the 172 community members who could conceivably be employed, 130 (equal numbers of men and women) currently work — most full time. This puts the employment rate for 'employable' adults at about 76%, but this figure is always on the rise. As children reach the age of 18, they are no longer eligible for Aid to Families with Dependent Children (AFDC), previously unemployed parents (primarily older widows) are forced to find jobs (Kirton, 1985: 90).

From all appearances, the La Playa Hmong have weathered the initial resettlement period well. People work, drive expensive cars, buy houses, and seem to be adjusting to their new life. However, it remains just that — a new life; precisely because the initial period is over, new problems, new conflicts, and new pressures emerge. We mentioned above the goals of United States government officials in managing the resettlement program — to control diseases, disperse the population, and encourage immediate self-sufficiency. Less emphasis has been given to one of the fundamental requirements for successful psychological and financial adjustment to a new country — effective communication skills.

Problems in Communication

More than successful adjustment to a new environment rests on host/refuge communication. English fluency makes adjustment to the United States faster and easier, but even basic survival depends on access to medical, educational, legal, vocational, and social services. For the majority of Hmong refugees, lack of fluency in English limits access to essential services; most Hmong receive services only with the help of an interpreter.

Arriving in the United States, Hmong experience the communication problems of other linguistic minorities. Like earlier arrivals, Hmong not fluent in English have trouble demanding their rights as tenants, patients, employees, and students. However, the ways in which Hmong cope with the majority language reflect particular features of their history and culture — details usually not understood by the host community.

Effective communication for receiving services in the host community has been a scarce resource in La Playa, for a number of reasons. First, decreased refugee funds eliminated paid interpreters. Second, the pattern of resettlement in La Playa created differential access to volunteer interpreters. Third, the host community did not give communication top priority. Finally, the host community, particularly school and medical personnel, and the Hmong community did not share the same ideas about the purpose of communication.

The Hmong as a Linguistic Minority

Living in a world of linguistic diversity has been a historical reality for the Hmong. The map shows no 'Hmongland'; whether Hmong live in China, Vietnam, Laos, Thailand, or the United States, they are linguistically and ethnically in the minority (see Halpern and Kunstadter, 1967). Some of the Hmong refugees who now find themselves in the United States struggling to communicate with an English-speaking majority, received their education in Lao, studied in French, and picked up bits and pieces of several of the other minority languages spoken in Laos. Unlike some other immigrant and refugee groups, Hmong are familiar with the experience of speaking one language at home and another at school, the hospital or the market place.

Individual Hmong experience the wide variety of languages spoken in Laos and the United States in different ways. A Hmong man old enough to have dealt with French colonialists may speak some French, read and write Laotian, know conversational Iu Mien and Khmu, and speak little English. A young woman of 23 is probably literate and fluent in Lao and English, but speaks neither French nor any member of the Laotian minority languages other than her own. Older women speak some Lao and less English, but rarely read either. Children educated in the United States lose Hmong as they learn English, and lack spoken and written Lao. Americans might be surprised to find that since arriving in the United States, any of these might be participating in Hmong literacy classes, taught by a community elder who has been literate in Hmong only since leaving Laos.

The Rise and Fall of Refugee Services

Although they arrived with a history as a linguistic minority, the communication needs of the Hmong in a new country were much more serious than they had been in Laos. Whereas many of the Hmong had some knowledge of the official language in Laos, few of those arriving in the United States could communicate in English. Furthermore, there was no escaping the need for English in all aspects of daily life, once Hmong stepped outside their apartment doors. Thus, the community depended on the services of Hmong interpreters for enrolling their children in school, getting basic medical care, buying cars, renting apartments, looking for jobs, and applying for welfare. In La Playa, Hmong interpreters were provided through the local resettlement agency, the Indochinese Project.

Ideally, refugee services grow in direct proportion to the size and needs of the community they serve. In this community, however, the two processes were not parallel. The resettlement agency began by providing multiple services to a small community, but funding, and thus services, decreased long before the refugee population declined. Programs in the schools, at the adult education ESL center, and at the ICP all received federal refugee funds and suffered with the reduction of refugee funding.

Loss of funds in 1981 affected programs nationwide, but hit La Playa particularly hard. As communities in California's central valley grew, La Playa no longer had enough refugees to compete for the limited federal assistance. Other funds, dependent on the number of welfare families, declined steadily as La Playa's employment rate rose.

With the loss of refugee funds, all the programs lost personnel. In 1981 the staff at the Indochinese Project dropped to four — director, secretary, Hmong employment counselor, and health clinic representative. No longer were interpreters available to help with medical and welfare appointments; from 1981 until its closing in 1984, the ICP provided vocational counseling only. After April 1984, no resettlement agency existed for Indochinese refugees in La Playa.

When formal services ceased in La Playa, community members and a local agency applied to the county for funds to establish an interpreter service. On an individual basis, Hmong asked for interpreters in welfare offices, hospitals, schools, and employment offices. All requests were denied on the basis of lack of funds — local, state, and federal. The county gave the refugee community (Lao and Vietnamese were also affected) the message that formal assistance had ended; the refugees were on their own.

Discontinuation of Paid Interpreters

As noted above, the interpreter crisis that began with the decrease in funding culminated with the elimination of formal services in 1984. At this point, refugees and service providers were left relying on interpreter services that could be arranged on a casual and seasonal basis.

Impetus for using informal interpreters came from both the host agencies and the Hmong residents. When American health care personnel initiated the use of the interpreter, they relied on the one remaining paid interpreter — the assistant to the public health nurse. Various young Hmong women (sometimes a high school student) filled the position at different times. Although she was technically an official interpreter employed by the county, the assistant's services were so limited by time (two hours daily) and by the scope of her job (making home visits, interpreting in the La Playa health office, and very occasionally accompanying a patient to a doctor's appointment) that she was not generally available to the community. Elementary and secondary schools had the option of calling on interpreters for specific problems. For instance, the elementary school hired an interpreter for parent conferences in the fall and for any problem they might have with students or parents at other times during the year.

Hmong also initiated the use of interpreters. Since Hmong normally did not pay for the services, however, they made more casual arrangements than the Americans. When they were lucky, Hmong called upon fluent English-speakers formerly employed in the Indochinese Project. However, access to the ex-ICP workers was unequal, and those without access to former interpreters relied on children. Those without children went without services.

Hmong Resettlement Workers

The details of resettlement in La Playa show the relationship between the process of resettlement and access to interpreters. As outlined above, the first Hmong to arrive in La Playa were the members of related patrilineages (Group I). The group included young educated men, literate in Lao, and fluent in English. The young men found almost immediate employment in the ICP, when it was established to assist refugees in getting health care, education, welfare benefits, and vocational training and placement. Since they were trilingual and could interpret for Lao as well as for Hmong refugees, their services were in constant demand. Members of the other group (Group II) arrived later in the resettlement process.

The two groups, Group I and Group II, differed in important ways. First, Group I had more members. Second, Group II did not have any representatives of their group working in the resettlement agency, primarily because of the lack of candidates of suitable age and education.

The fact that Group II had no members employed in the resettlement agency affected their access to services from the start of resettlement. In theory, of course, all residents have equal access to services of a public agency. In practice, however, community dynamics interfered with that access.

In resettlement, just as in Laos, lineage and clan connections are fundamental to Hmong life. While agency interpreters clearly did not restrict themselves to serving members of their own families, it would be naive to ignore the importance of lineage and clan connections. This was particularly true when services had been reduced but not yet eliminated.

During this period, the interpreter/counselor's official duties covered only vocational assistance — trying to place refugees in employment by contacting employers and accompanying clients to job interviews. The interpreter had some leeway as to how he spent his work time, and he frequently had the opportunity to extend his services beyond the employment scene. Rather than being obligated to help all those applying to the agency, however, he alone decided how, when, and to whom he would offer help. Hmong from Group II complained that the ICP worker (himself a member of Group I) consistently refused to help Group II Hmong with medical and welfare interpreting.

Concurrent with the decrease in established resettlement services was a growing frustration among the young men active in the development of the La Playa Hmong community. Having worked for years as liaisons and interpreters, they gradually scaled down service provision for all but close relatives.

Thus, with the elimination of the formal refugee services, the resources available to the Hmong in Group I remained constant for most families, while Group II Hmong were largely without resources. In spite of occasional exceptions, Group II Hmong had fewer options than Group I Hmong.

During the decline and discontinuation of refugee services, American service providers did not recognize differences within the Hmong community. Still seeing the community as homogeneous, still overlooking regional, educational, and family differences, Americans working with Hmong were unaware that individual families varied in their ability to draw upon family resources and in their need for outside assistance. Americans were unaware that in spite of the fact that many young Hmong still performed interpreting and other services for family members, Hmong in Group II did not have equal access to these favors. Americans frequently attributed to the Hmong community more solidarity than actually existed.

Children as Interpreters

In the absence of paid interpreters, service providers in La Playa and the larger community placed the burden of communication on the Hmong.

Except in rather serious and isolated instances, Americans held Hmong responsible for arranging for interpreters to talk to school personnel, seek medical care, and apply for welfare.

When competent adult interpreters were unavailable, parents and service providers turned to the children. The use of children had its most serious effect in medical situations. Presumably, medical personnel preferred relying on children than demanding that the county provide paid interpreters. Parents, on the other hand, had no other options. Whether understandable or not, using children as interpreters placed an unfair burden on them and decreased the possibility for effective communication, particularly in the area of health care. The following examples illustrate the frustration of Hmong parents and children dealing with American medical personnel.

An 11-year-old girl missed school regularly to interpret for her father's medical appointments. The girl, her mother, and her father went frequently, spending hours on the bus and waiting in the clinic. The father's physical complaints persisted for an entire year. Worried about her grades, the girl told her parents she needed to stay at school, but they had no one else to ask. At the appointments, the doctor doubted that the symptoms were real; he questioned the daughter, asking her if she thought her father could be faking illness (Kirton, 1987).

A girl of 12 worried about her mother's refusal to follow the diet prescribed to control her diabetes. The doctor had scolded the daughter, saying that her mother would be dead in five years if she did not comply. Hearing the brutal consequences, the girl felt responsible and frightened about her mother's actions — actions over which she had no control (Kirton, 1987).

A 16-year-old boy accompanied his father to the hospital to hear the explanation of the emergency appendectomy to be performed on a family member. Because of the son's presence, the nurse felt confident that the surgery consent was 'informed'. The father understood nothing of the medical explanation. Both father and son had both been too embarrassed to admit their confusion. When a competent interpreter (also a family member) called the hospital for the diagnosis and details, the nurse and doctor refused to discuss the case, saying they had already gone over everything with the 'interpreter' (Kirton, 1987).

As is clear from these examples, Hmong children may seem bilingual to parents and medical personnel, but they lack the language and sophistication adults require of them. Parents assume that children whose English skills enable them to communicate at school, the store, and with the housing manager would also understand medical terminology. Most

Hmong parents have no way of knowing that the language used by the medical profession is beyond the sophistication of even American-born, English-speaking children. Doctors, although they should know better, rely, just as strongly as the parents do, on the children's ability to understand medical language.

Parents, unlike medical personnel, at least recognized the gaps in their children's knowledge of their native language. As children progress in the American school system and watch American television, they become more familiar with American conceptions of illness than with their parents' beliefs. No longer able to relate to traditional ideas about what causes and cures illness, and either having forgotten or never having learned critical vocabulary, children are at a loss to communicate their parents' symptoms to the doctors. When children do not ask questions, doctors end the communication.

Beyond the assumptions about language, both parents and medical personnel had unreasonable expectations of what children can do in adult situations. Parents expect children to be their advocates — questioning, complaining, and fighting for adequate care. They ask their children to withhold information and to hide family secrets from disapproving Americans. Medical personnel, on the other hand, expect children to elicit from their parents complete descriptions of symptoms that would be indiscreet to discuss across gender and generational boundaries. Doctors and nurses expect children to be able to relay the seriousness of instructions and exert influence on their parents to comply.

Those with access to neither adult nor child interpreters simply do without. When all goes well, this results merely in an amusing situation in the doctor's office, with doctor and patients relying on pantomime, friendliness, and humor. Too often, however, the lack of access to interpreters in routine and emergency situations has more serious consequences.

For instance, a cancer patient lay in the hospital for months with only intermittent help from English-speaking relatives. Although they participated as much as their schedules permitted, they knew too little English to help the patient find out what the diagnosis was and when she would be released. She waited from day to day, unable to communicate her fear, her pain, and the varying effects of the medications (Kirton, 1985: 166).

Children, victims of illnesses that go untreated, suffer the consequences. Having recently moved to another location, a young mother hesitated to take her sick child to the doctor. By the time the parents went to seek help, the child had died from complications due to chicken pox —

something virtually unheard of with modern medical care (Kirton, 1987). Another child suffered permanent liver damage when his parents, newly arrived from Thailand, knew little about getting medical care (Kirton, 1985: 121).

Stories of delayed treatment because of communication problems abound. As frequent consumers of health care, women in the community are particularly susceptible to delayed care. Knowing they will not be able to communicate their objections to Caesarean births, episiotomies, and rupturing the amniotic sac, women wait as long as possible before going to the hospital to deliver — sometimes until the baby arrives. In response to a question about her opinion of American hospital deliveries, one woman answered, 'You don't know the language, so you just lie still. They do what they want, and you just lie still' (Kirton, 1987).

Communication in the Schools

Nowhere are the problems of communication more apparent than in local schools. Hmong children adjust to life in the United States in a variety of contexts. Their adjustment takes place within the school environment, within the Hmong community, and within the larger host community. The success of the children's adjustment to American schools depends in part on the relationship between home and school. However, little is known by either about the other, and chances for effective communication between home and school are slim. For the schools and other local agencies, the Hmong remain a cultural enigma. For most Hmong families the American school is equally unfamiliar. Hmong children move from one sphere to another, interpreting (literally and figuratively) the culture of home to the school and the culture of school to the home.

Many Americans working with Hmong children are unaware of the individual differences in the community. They rely, instead, on the tried and true generalizations perpetuated by the press. While teachers spread the word that the Hmong have no written language, Hmong children see adults writing Hmong in three different scripts — one using the Romanized Popular Alphabet, one using Lao script, and the third developed and perpetuated by Hmong. While children hear in the larger community that Hmong did not go to school before they came to the United States, they hear Hmong adults describe the family sacrifices made for access to the limited educational opportunities in Laos.

On the other hand, the picture most Hmong adults have of American schools is no less clouded by misunderstandings. While the idea of 'school' was familiar and valued in pre-resettlement Hmong life, clearly, most Hmong had limited exposure to the actual classroom activities of reading, writing, and math.

This lack of widespread experience combines with language problems to convince parents that they do not know and will not understand what teachers teach and children learn. Teachers frequently compound the lack of understanding with conference explanations focusing on 'reading comprehension', 'inferential comprehension', and 'computational skills'.

When asked for questions at the end of the parent-teacher conference, the most frequent Hmong reply is, '*Kuv ruam ruam.*' The translation is, 'I am stupid,' and alternatively, 'I am mute.' Explaining why he had no questions, one father went on to say,

> I don't know anything. I can't do anything to help my child learn at school. Tell the teacher thank you for helping my child and please to continue to help. I leave everything to the teacher (Kirton, 1987).

Because they have the money to pay for interpreters, school personnel control the timing and the content of school/home communication. During our research, one of the researchers (Kirton, 1985) was asked by one of the junior high schools to interpret for a parent conference to discuss severe problems teachers had with a 14-year-old girl. The scene played out in the school conference room illustrates the cultural conflict experienced by Hmong parents as they try to facilitate the education of their children.

Having heard that schools in one part of the county used an American interpreter to deal with Hmong parents, one of the teachers called to arrange a conference. She explained that all the girl's teachers found her a mystery in the classroom. She behaved radically different from any of the other Hmong children in the school, refused to participate in most activities, frequently ignored her assignments, and did not seem to have any friends — even of the Hmong children.

The teacher arranged a meeting between the girl's parents, her resource teacher, the principal, her counselor, the school psychologist, and the public health nurse. When they had agreed on the day and time, the teacher told the interpreter she would send a note home to tell the parents when to appear. She did not mention asking the parents' permission to use this particular interpreter, nor did she explain to the parents the reason for the conference.

The interpreter suggested a more personal approach. Since she had never met the parents, she suggested calling a friend to introduce her to the family, then going early on the day of the conference to meet with the parents, explain the conference, and drive them to the school.

Arriving at the family's apartment, the interpreter attracted attention. Although American visitors from the church and the welfare department came from time to time, they did not ask directions from the children in Hmong. Hmong, who had moved from La Playa to the neighboring town, leaned out of their windows, called greetings to the interpreter, and directed her to the correct apartment.

After chatting with the parents and a daughter-in-law briefly, the interpreter explained the reason she had been called. The parents were also concerned about the girl's behavior; she did not behave normally around other Hmong, she complained that she had no friends, and she said that the American children made fun of her. The interpreter explained that her role was to help the parents communicate; if they had thoughts, questions, or comments to express to the teachers, she would be their mouth.

On the way to the school, the parents relaxed and chatted about other times they had been at the school. There had been other calls from Hmong students acting as interpreters, telling them to come in for a conference.

The meeting lasted two-and-a-half hours, during which the teachers presented their concerns, asked questions, and requested that the parents help them improve the girl's behavior. They had noticed a growing unhappiness in the girl and hoped to pinpoint something that might have happened to cause a deterioration in her school performance.

Although the meeting was too long to detail, the questions asked by the teachers and those asked by the parents showed completely different concerns. The psychologist was worried that the parents were contributing to low self-esteem, since in another conference, the student interpreter translated the mother's statement that her daughter was not a good student, not pretty, and, in fact, not special in any way. In fact, this is the only appropriate response for a parent to give. Even the parents of the school's top students will express surprise and disagreement, saying, 'Well, she's not smart — she has to do the best she can.'

One of the teachers thought the girl might have been forced to get married. Another thought she might be unhappy that she was *not* married, since a few of the school's students had married in their last year of junior high school. They also worried that maybe the girl was overburdened by the housekeeping demands made by her parents.

Both parents spoke at length. In fact, they had so many questions and explanations, that the other participants left, one by one, until only the parents, the interpreter, and one teacher remained. They worried as well, but about different matters. First, they discussed their daughter's reports of being ridiculed by American children about her Asian appearance. The principal dismissed this, saying he had joked with the girl about *his* homeliness, when she got sent to his office to discuss her lack of cooperation at school.

Second, they were anxious to plan for their daughter's future. They were afraid that she had not attended the proficiency examination; would this be a problem in the future? When the teacher brushed the importance of the exam aside, the mother persisted. The reason for her concern, she said, was that the girl was her only child. Who would take care of her in her old age if her daughter did not do well enough in school to secure steady employment?

The school personnel quickly side-stepped the matter of the future. They returned to specific behavior, how it was not acceptable in school, and what they could do to remedy it. For the Hmong, however, education appears to be absolute insurance for financial security. Without it, their children will be unable to succeed.

Third, the mother wanted to investigate the possibility of medical problems. She said that she had been worried over her daughter's behavior for a long time, and wondered if they could take X-rays of her brain to see if something were wrong. This was the single area on which the school personnel and the parents agreed.

At the end of the meeting, two agreements had been made. The public health nurse would begin the paperwork necessary to request approval from Medi-Cal for diagnostic tests, and the school would call the mother for another conference at the end of the year. This request was made by the mother, as was the request that the interpreter/researcher again be called for the conference.

When the last week of school arrived, the school had not yet contacted the interpreter for the conference. After inquiring, she found that the conference had been held, with the interpreter for the public health nurse present. The mother and the teacher had both wanted the interpreter/researcher, the teacher said, but it was assumed she was 'busy'. During the summer the girl was hospitalized with seizures. When she was released, Hmong community members reported that the mother had never understood what was wrong with her daughter. The school reported that a final conference had been held with the mother, at which the daughter had interpreted.

Conclusion

Clearly, schools and other agencies providing services to Hmong refugees also suffer from the cultural conflict and the barriers to effective communication. For Americans, the communication problems can be left at work, while for the Hmong, the Lao, or any other underserved linguistic minority, the problem is never left behind. The words of a Hmong father poignantly illustrate the dramatic division between the Hmong world and that of their American neighbors. He said:

> Long ago our great-grandmothers and great-grandfathers came to Laos from China. We have lived in Laos for seven generations. When we came to make our home in Laos there was no fighting, no war. There was no hunger and no thirst. We had animals; we had rice. We had food to eat and water to drink, and we envied no one. We lived this way for seven generations, until 1960. Then the war began. When General Vang Pao went to Long Cheng, we went too. We stayed until 1975. On May 14, we left. We abandoned our homes and our fields. We left our cows and our buffalo. Everything we had, we left behind. What we had was good, and we had to leave it all. Now I am afraid that we will leave our history, our customs, and our traditions behind as well. There are other people, people who are more clever than we are. If they have something important to remember, they simply write it on paper. We Hmong, however, have no writing. Whatever we want to remember, to keep, we must say as I am telling you now. If no one talks about our history, about our traditions, they will disappear. We have lost our country, we have lost our fields, and I am afraid that our way of life is over. Whether it is good or bad, no one will know. Now we live in America, and we don't speak their language. Americans are more powerful than we are. Because we are quiet like the monkeys and the gibbons, maybe Americans think we are a people with no history, with no past. Americans don't come to visit us. Their letters come to us, but it isn't that they want to see us or talk to us. Their letters come asking for the rent or for the phone bill or for the electricity bill. Listen to my words and tell the Americans that we have a history; we have a past. We had a way of life that was good, but we lost our country. If we hadn't lost our country, we wouldn't have come to live here (Kirton, 1985: 33–34).

Chapter four

Becoming American through Schooling

From the preceding chapters, we can see that the experiences of the Hmong in the United States are yet another chapter in their continuing history of minority status. It is also important to note that many of the initial resettlement locations turned out to be temporary stops in the continued migration of the Hmong, as they looked for hospitable areas within America. For many families, La Playa was only a stopover while moving from the Midwest to California. Although La Playa provided warmer weather, the constant rent increases in the area forced many Hmong to move again to other towns and cities. Even as this book is being written, Hmong families are moving from La Playa to other locations, looking for cheaper housing, better opportunities, and a stronger sense of community.

In America, as in Laos, a sense of community has held great importance to the Hmong. The 'community' includes formal and informal relationships and networks. The formal leadership has transferred from Laos to the United States, but Hmong still defer to traditional elders from long standing family lineages. Also as in Laos, the extended family continues to have enormous importance. It is the natural unit responsible for the entire welfare of each individual, as well as the economic and social unit for the collective survival of all members. Furthermore, the family is also the cultural center which explains survival, cohesiveness and endurance of Hmong people in the face of adversity.

Through existing folktales and oral history, these values can be clearly seen. The family has the important function of socializing and enculturating new members into Hmong history and folklore. Until thirty years ago there was no writing system for the Hmong language; much of the culture is still transmitted orally. As grandparents tell and retell stories and tales of the Hmong, they are also passing along their view of the world, their values, traditions and lifestyle. These values have survived through domination in Laos, degrading experiences in refugee camps in Thailand, and are now sometimes in conflict with the new standards of American culture.

To understand the home life of the Hmong refugee families, it helps to know these folktales. In the stories, themes regarding marriage, fair treatment of family members, sharing, and becoming rich are quite common. Attention to these topics remains high among contemporary Hmong people, who now face the challenge of integrating traditional values with those of our industrial, Western, American society.

School in Laos

Families reported that, generally, in Laos only the boys attended school, and often only one son from each family. They were farmers, help was needed with the crops, and school was seen as a luxury. The father of a Hmong student in the local school explained that when he lived in Laos he was a farmer and

> ...did not have the opportunity to attend school, although I wished I had. I felt the obligation to work my family's land because my own father was dead, my brother was a soldier, and my sister was married (Jacobs, 1986).

To those who attended school in Laos, as well as those that did not, American schools were viewed as 'very good', compared to schools in Laos. This was not so much because of the quality of instruction, which most parents could not assess, but because American teachers were perceived as more humane. One father said,

> In Laos children get hit hard with a ruler if they don't behave. And they also have to kneel on rocks for a long time if they are bad. It hurts. Our children hear stories about this, and they are glad they don't go to school in Laos (Jacobs, 1986).

Other families confirmed these feelings and described similar practices. A mother related this information:

> In Laos, the teachers are so mean to the children that parents worry about the safety of their children when they are in school. When a student misbehaves, the teacher makes a friend inflict the punishment. If the friend hits too soft then they would also get in trouble (Jacobs, 1986).

The memory of teacher cruelty in Laotian schools had a definite impact on another mother who became sad as she described the experience of her brother.

> My brother went to school in the city, and the teachers were so mean and they would hit so hard that he would come home crying. That is why he went to be a soldier, and he was killed. Even though our kids haven't gone to school there, we tell them that the teachers here are so nice that even if you don't wash your face or anything, the teachers are still happy to hug you and talk to you (Jacobs, 1986).

Thus, we can see that memories from Laos of the physical and mental anguish that many Hmong suffered made parents predisposed to be satisfied with American schools. Furthermore, the high status of teachers in Laos made criticism impossible, and a critical view of educational practices is not easily developed even years after relocation.

In Refugee Camps

For most of the Hmong in La Playa, the interim between leaving Laos and entering refugee camps in Thailand consisted of a difficult and treacherous journey. As they went on foot, under cover of the night, across the mountains and the Mekong River, people experienced hardship, fear, danger and death. Unfortunately, arriving at the 'safety' of the border camps did not really end the trauma. The Hmong were subject to further degrading experiences by the guards in charge, to a breakdown in social order as food became scarce, to robbery, rape, and the constant state of uncertainty.

Due to connections or past experiences, however, some people had unique experiences. A man in the La Playa community had a higher command of the English language and was more sophisticated in his behavior because he had been exposed to the American culture and had been associated with American people at work. Feeling that a war was imminent and not wanting to fight, he had left Laos earlier than most other refugees and had gone to Thailand. There, he worked for an American company, whose boss sent him to school to learn English.

Some time later he left his job and returned to his village in Laos to find a bride. After the wedding he brought his wife to a refugee camp in Thailand and they applied for American visas. In order to facilitate the process he needed papers proving that he had worked for an American company. Travelling with documents associating Hmong with Americans was dangerous at that time, so he no longer had the documents. They did not want to wait in the refugee camp, so, in order to avoid delay, they bought documents showing affiliation with an American company from a Lao family which was not planning to emigrate to the United States. This hastened their departure, and the family kept the Lao name even after immigrating to the United States rather than be considered illegal aliens.

In the US clinicians, working with Hmong clients exhibiting post-traumatic stress disorders, state that the refugees are dealing not only with residue from the escape journey, but also from the constant need for survival skills in the refugee camps. The lack of stability or safety has over time built up certain behaviors that are deeply internalized.

Primary Resettlement Experiences

Although La Playa was a primary resettlement site, much of the growth of the community resulted from secondary migration. Some of the families came to La Playa telling of conflicts they experienced with church sponsors in other areas, such as Minnesota and Wisconsin. One student's family landed in Minnesota where their host family lived. The cold weather was a hardship for which they were unprepared, but the most serious difficulty they encountered was the way in which their sponsors tried to dictate their lives. Their sponsor would deposit their checks in a saving account and give them only a small amount to meet the most urgent expenses. They did not get enough money even to buy food, and for the first winter they subsisted mainly on potatoes. At first, they were uncertain about their rights and, as they did not understand their relationship to their sponsors, they decided to tolerate the situation for a while. Later, other Hmong refugees told them they could have access to the money themselves and move to California, which they did.

For the families that moved to California, the climate was improved, but other difficulties remained. The lack of housing and work continued to be the most serious obstacles to permanent settlement. Circumstances forced children to switch schools many times, prolonging their adjustment period and the situation of being newcomers. Thus, the difficulties of readjustment continued: new situations demanded new activities and support systems, the gap between generations widened, and degrading experiences continued to have a strong impact on many Hmong refugees.

Home Environments in La Playa

In the town of La Playa, refugee families were still on the move — owing to high rents, weather conditions, employment, and family concerns. The number of Hmong in La Playa was continuously decreasing, as one community member eloquently stated, 'A lot of Hmong have lived here for over five years and they love this town. But they have to go. They have jobs, they have kids in school, but they can't pay the rent. They say, "I don't want to go!" But they have no choice' (Jacobs, 1986).

The families in La Playa were divided into renters and home owners. By joining together, some families had been able to combine income and buy homes. Often this resulted in two or three families living in one house, each household having a bedroom and using the living room and kitchen communally. Hmong culture is patrilineal, and sons are responsible for taking care of the parents. This custom persists strongly today, and many families include the husband's parents or parent, since many men had died in the war.

Visits to Hmong families' houses revealed cultural differences beyond the obvious ones of clothing and language. The use of space was in distinct contrast to a mainstream American household. In one apartment, seven people lived together in a one bedroom apartment — a woman, her husband and his mother, and four children. The use of space was determined according to need. Usually the grandmother and the older daughter shared the bedroom, with all the others rolling out bedding in the living room nightly.

> Entering this family's home, I was instantly struck by the smallness of the area and the amount of people and things inside it. Four plastic straight back chairs stood in a row against one wall, and opposite them was an old couch covered by a sheet where one of the younger girls was napping. Bedding was rolled up against the kitchen counter, and in every available space there were folded clothes, boxes, fishing gear, extra lamps, pots, and pans. On the walls were Hmong calendars, the children's good behavior certificates from school, and class photos. Near the window, in the fading afternoon light, the grandmother squatted, working on her embroidery. Wearing a fluorescent green ski hat and two sweaters, she painstakingly made the intricate stitching for squares of 'pa ndao' [embroidered cloth] which the family sold at street fairs (Jacobs, 1986).

About a block away, another family lived in a second story apartment. When I visited this home, six adults were sitting around a color TV. The blond lady on the screen smiled broadly as the commentator spoke of the benefits of Crest toothpaste. An old grandmother, monolingual in Hmong, sat to the left of the screen, oblivious to the message of the commercial. Giving a small child her baby-bottle, the grandma smiled fondly, revealing — in contrast to the woman on television — about six yellow teeth with gaping spaces in between (Jacobs, 1986).

Another boy lived in a two bedroom apartment with eight other people — including his parents, two brothers, two sisters, another unrelated man and the man's son. After struggling to meet the high rents in La Playa, the family decided they would move to another city at the end of the school year. They had no friends there, but the town had a growing Hmong community. 'There is a Hmong store there,' the parents told me, while in La Playa, the two Indochinese stores were both owned by Vietnamese families. Rents were more affordable in the other city as well. In La Playa their rent was over $1000 per month.

The family of Song, a third grade girl, lived in a rented three bedroom duplex on the back streets of La Playa, shared with two other families of her father's brothers. Two brothers had settled there together, and the third family came following the death of the third brother from 'SUNDS' (sudden unexplained nocturnal death syndrome), which causes the deaths of many young Hmong men for no apparent reason. Altogether, there were twenty people in the home. The immediate family consisted of her parents and seven children. Each family had only one bedroom, but the garage had been turned into a bedroom for the two older sisters. Needless to say, the house was crowded, noisy, and sometimes tense.

Compared with other children and community members, one 9-year-old boy had a unique family situation. Just two children and their parents occupied the three bedroom home. Church members had given the father a job at their printing office where he became manager. His serious responsibilities required long hours on a daily basis. The father liked his work, and felt the extra hours he put into the job were required both by the business and by his own financial situation. Since there were no relatives living with the family, he had to meet the high mortgage payments by himself. He felt that owning a house was the only way to survive in America (Jacobs, 1986).

These examples illustrate that there is not just one typical home-life for Hmong refugees, but a whole spectrum of lifestyles influenced by degrees of successful adaptation to American mainstream society. The different pace in adaptation is revealed not only across families but even within families. These differences may be somewhat related to varying degrees of exposure to, and understanding of, American culture.

Lifestyles and Concerns

Children are a focal point of the integration of cultures. They move in and out of home and school environments that are in sharp contrast to each other. While school-age children are exposed to American values and culture at school, at church, and from contact with their peers, parents must have a certain income level, as well as a minimum communicative competence in order to participate in the new social institutions and adopt an American lifestyle. In an effort to break their isolation parents often attend ESL programs and church activities, but grandparents generally do not participate in these activities. Thus, the elders and the youngest children, who are cared for by them, are left behind in the process of 'Americanization'. The youngsters will soon face the challenge of school; the grandparents remain outside the system.

A community elder, who had been a military official in Laos, spoke of how the community as a whole attempted to acquire American culture and fit into American society. Formally and informally, Hmong heads of household encouraged members of the family to dress American, to learn English, and to not do anything that would bring negative attention to the community. Although the elder acknowledged the necessity of assimilation, he also expressed concern about the children's increasing loss of Hmong language and culture, and their lack of familiarity with Hmong history. Reflecting on this he said, 'Some of the children, and some of the older people do not know who came from where; who came from China and who were the first people here. I think it is important for people to know' (Jacobs, 1986).

While there were important ethnic, social, economic differences in La Playa Hmong families, there were also significant common linguistic and cultural characteristics. In the Hmong refugee community, the main responsibility of the family as a cohesive sociocultural and economic unit had been, and continued to be, the survival of all its members in very basic terms: food, shelter, safety and health. Their concerns with high rents, medical treatment, limited income, access to essential information (through translation) and transportation continue to be at the top of the family priority lists.

Households almost always included members of the extended family, which made sense financially, because it saved money in rent and food.

Maximizing the use of money provided extended family members with some sort of insurance protecting individuals whose employment was not secure. They knew well that at least some adults of the family were employed only part of the time. With more wage earners there was more money to pay the high rents or even to purchase a house and afford the mortgage payments. Grandparents who could not get jobs took care of the younger children and did some domestic chores while parents were at work. Most adults in the La Playa community were employed by the local electronics companies, working on the assembly line during either the day or night shift. Consequently, many parents were unable to be with their children immediately before or after school hours. Parents took those jobs realizing that there are few advancement possibilities for them and often said, 'I can go no further. But my children will do better.'

Daily schedules were very demanding and reflected the impact that employment of both parents had on the family. The day began at dawn when the mother, or another woman, made a communal breakfast. The parent who worked day shift often had to be at work by six a.m. The remaining parent, adult relative, or the older children prepared the other youngsters for school. Hmong children generally were the first to arrive at the playground, having started their day earlier than most of their classmates. Mothers who did not have a job, or who worked at night, took care of young children — their own as well as those of relatives — at home. Women were always busy at home embroidering, cooking, and gardening. During the day men participated in child-care and gardening activities, but they also went hunting and fishing when they had the time.

On week-ends adults attended Bible study classes at their local church where there were also classes for children. Besides church activities, families often went as a group to local ranches in order to pick fruit or to buy a pig for slaughter and to share. There were also soccer games for the men. Some families traveled to other cities in California to visit relatives or attend family celebrations, such as wedding ceremonies (Kirton, 1987).

The home language of the families was Hmong, but 'American' — as they called English — was used by Hmong children when they didn't want their parents to understand what they said. During the first years of relocation many adults attended ESL classes and made progress in the use of the English language. As people became employed they gave their work priority, which often conflicted with ESL class attendance, and language classes had to be dropped. It was difficult for adults to continue learning language once they entered the work force. Hmong children, although they did not find the English language as difficult as Hmong adults, still had serious problems learning English when they began school. Beyond the acquisition of new language forms, children and adults had to acquire a new way of viewing reality — a way in clear contrast to that of their parents and grandparents. The full impact of this realization does not come in the first months, or even the first years after arrival. It is only over a long period of time that the cultural conflict between a Hmong conception of life and the American view of the world comes into a clear perspective for the young Hmong people.

The Hmong community's acceptance of American commodities — such as automobiles and televisions — sometimes makes it appear as if this reflects a total acceptance of the new culture. In fact, there is a selective acceptance of some aspects of American culture and a rejection of others. For example, some weddings, which have been influenced by American culture, are no longer arranged by the parents, and may take place in the church. However, many marriages are arranged and conducted according to Hmong customs. The traditional value placed on marriage, and the significant clan linkages resulting from it, are still very important in Hmong life.

La Playa Hmong with church affiliations were well acquainted with the American disapproval of teenage marriages. Nevertheless, early marriage was still a common practice. However, it was often kept secret until the girl turned 18. Consequently, many young women who became pregnant were stigmatized as single teen-mothers by the school authorities, but they were seen by the Hmong as perfectly normal within cultural tradition. This is a very sensitive topic, and has resulted in tension between American authorities and service providers and the Hmong community.

The following example from field notes by Jacobs in 1986 illustrates Hmong marriage practices and the cultural conflict inherent in their transition from traditional arrangements to American practices. Chang, a teenage Hmong girl at La Playa school, had excelled in her academic work and became very close to a teacher who acted as her mentor. When Chang graduated from elementary school, this teacher helped her secure a scholarship to an excellent private middle school and arranged for her to stay with an American family during the week. Chang's mother, who was a widow and had three other children, agreed to this arrangement, but there was some disapproval by other community members. Chang did well in middle school and spent some time volunteering at the local hospital in a school-related program. Working with American doctors impressed her, especially seeing the success of surgeries. Chang had seen many people die in Laos and Thailand, and after her hospital experience she expressed a desire to become a doctor in order to help people.

Then, unexpectedly, due to a rent increase, her family was forced to leave the area. Chang had to join them in the new location. After completing a year of high school, and under pressure, she married a man chosen by her mother. Her mother felt that this man was the best choice because he was of her clan and was a college graduate. Chang's mother was afraid that if she waited any longer, he would marry someone else, and her daughter might have to marry a man from another clan. Chang cried throughout the marriage ceremony. Afterwards, the couple moved to another state where the groom had been living (Jacobs, 1986). Subsequently, when the welfare department found out about the circumstances of the wedding, questions arose regarding Chang's consent to marry. The marriage had been conducted as a Hmong ceremony only, and therefore it was not recognized by American law. Chang reappeared and stated that she was not married. Chang and her secret husband than moved in with her mother so she could continue attending school. They planned to leave town after the authorities lost interest in their case.

The custom of the groom giving a bride payment to the bride's family also persisted and ranged in price from about one to five thousand dollars. This practice had mixed implications and opinions about it vary. Some women felt it insured them a certain value, others felt it continued the idea that the bride was owned by the husband. The psychological effect of this was sometimes manifested by women, who expressed hopelessness in that they had no choice regarding what happened in their lives. The bride price also had implications for divorce; it needed to be considered in view of the possibility of losing this large payment.

Some customs and beliefs were challenged by a gap between what was accepted in the context of Hmong culture, but at the same time was not included as legitimate in American culture. Some people solved the dilemma by adjusting their views to the different acceptable realities. For example, when speaking about ghosts one boy said, 'Here there aren't any, but in Laos there are spirits from the dead people.' His mother explained further,

> We never saw any, but the old people said that you had to be really careful how you talked. If you were sick and afterwards you said you were better, if a ghost heard that, they would come back and make you sick again. So you had better say, 'I'm a little better.' If you say, 'I'm better — no problem', then it's not good. A lot of time when you got sick there was no hospital to go to so people said that it was ghosts. But now there are hospitals so they don't believe it any more (Jacobs, 1986).

Conversations of this sort remained puzzling. It was never clear whether Hmong people felt it necessary to disavow certain beliefs when speaking to Americans, or if they really did not accept old traditions. Many Hmong were reluctant to admit to their American friends, who were mainly church connected, that they still believed in spirits or traditional medicine. This did not stop them, however, from travelling to another community in search of herbs and traditional curing rituals when Western medicine did not seem to help.

Parents' perceptions of what actually happens in American schools were vague. The educational backgrounds of parents and their school experiences in Laos had little in common with those of their children in our public schools. It was not only a problem of attitude, or the internalization of parental roles, or even the lack of English that constrained Hmong parents in dealing with schools; it was also their realistic awareness of the very profound social and cultural differences between school personnel and themselves. Most parents did not have a concrete idea of what their children did or learned in American classrooms and invested the schools with a magical power to teach the children, '. . . everything there is to know'. Although parents verbally supported the importance of school, they had little substantial knowledge to ascertain what kind of specific help their children needed in order to be successful in the educational process. As one mother said, 'If you don't know yourself, and if you don't know how to help them, you just hope that the teachers will help them. You just hope that the teachers will help them and teach them everything they can and encourage them to go to school' (Jacobs, 1986).

Goals for their children were often vaguely defined. One mother said, 'I feel my children can be anything they want, I just don't know what there is to be.' Another said: 'I want my daughter to learn until she knows, so that she will be able to get a job that will be enough for her to eat' (Jacobs, 1986).

Parents still operated from the perspective of their social and cultural background, often without the benefits of literacy skills in any language. Refugee families learned to survive wars, hunger, and cultural shock in Laos, Thailand and the U.S. by holding onto their cultural values and securing with determination food, shelter and safety. Now that they are 'settled' they are asked to learn to adjust to American life. Situations demand that they integrate new cultural values, particularly those associated with literacy and school achievement, into their lives.

Children were as unfamiliar with what their parents did for a living as parents were with the work children did in school. While parents' actual jobs might be unknown to children, nevertheless children were aware of parents' special skills recognized in the Hmong community. A boy, for example, knew that his father was well respected as an expert in massage and healing, but he never mentioned this to his teacher when asked what his father did. Apparently he had internalized the difference in cultural values between his home community and the school.

La Playa Elementary School

The La Playa Elementary School is located in a university community in Southern California. The neighborhood it serves is a beach community composed largely of students, transients, low income and some mainstream families. Children of students and professors, as well as those of the recent refugee populations attend the school. In 1986 the La Playa school population was 591 students, half of whom spoke a first language other than English; twenty-five languages were represented, Spanish being the largest group (101), and Hmong being the next (77).

Special programs offered by the school include reading and language labs, a learning disability resource program, and a Spanish/English bilingual education. Part-time aides, funded by Title I grants, are used in the classrooms, to work with children that are performing below grade level. During certain times of the year, there are also student teachers from the university credential program. Two psychological counselors are on site one day per week; neither is bilingual or has had crosscultural training. The majority of school personnel are Anglo, the exceptions being Hispanic teachers in the bilingual program. There are no Asian adults employed by the school.

Other than talking about school back in Laos, parents did not often talk about school at all. Often it was the older siblings who were asked to assist students with their homework. Although brothers and sisters expressed concern, they also said they had no time to help. One student who was doing poorly in school was a cause of worry to his elder brother. Attending the community college and working kept him away from home most of the time, so he asked his parents to help. They were more than willing, but they felt inadequate to help with the schoolwork.

During one semester families reported that they met with the teachers only once. Furthermore, they could not really communicate, since the parents were limited in English, and there were no translators. Thus, not much was accomplished. One boy's father remembered the teacher telling him that his son had trouble reading, but he did not know what to do with that information other than to agree. Subsequently, the teacher recorded the parent's response as a negative one. On the school record, this was described in a brief sentence, 'Parents did not react'. Obviously parents did not know how to react; the language and cultural barriers made any reaction impossible.

Another man, more familiar with English, told his son's teacher that he did not understand the report card. The teacher then used this as an example of the only parent who ever admitted to her his lack of understanding, and that the other parents just said 'yes' to everything. This teacher did not realize that this father's disclosure was a function of his level of cultural and linguistic sophistication, and that the absence of inquiries on the part of other Hmong parents was not a sign of disinterest. Parents were often unable to communicate what they needed to know, and were not familiar enough with the American culture to assess the appropriateness of their questions. In fact, their socialization prior to coming to this country often persuaded them that it was totally inappropriate to ask questions.

Parents emphasized the need for more direct communication between the Hmong people and the school personnel in order that the parents better understand how to help their children, and that the school understand the needs of the Hmong community. A Hmong mother expressed her dissatisfaction this way, 'The only time the teachers and the principal talk to me is when they want embroidery.'

Discussing how youngsters would handle problems that might come up at school, a junior high girl explained that if there was trouble at school, Hmong students would not tell their parents. She also made it clear that the concept of 'having problems' is not in the Hmong perception of school.

'Hmong children do not talk to their parents about if they like school or their teachers. They do not think about things in that way. They don't think about things as problems. If something is bothering them they would tell a friend, not their parents. Hmong kids are not like that close to their parents. They don't share like private stuff with them. If you talk to your mom and dad, most of the parents just say "forget it" or something' (Jacobs, 1986).

Cultural Conflict and Stress

This same teenager gave this advice for younger Hmong students, and revealed some of her own conflict as well.

'Some Hmong kids are shy and all they hang around with are Hmong people. They are shy to speak up in classes and stuff. Maybe they should get in there like the American kids and start talking in class and stuff. I think that if when they are young they get involved with other kids that maybe when they get older they will be less scared and shy. Sometimes I think to myself that I wish I didn't know my language and just knew English so I wouldn't be confused. But on the other side I think about my culture and keeping it' (Jacobs, 1986).

She eloquently stated the difficulty of being caught in the middle between two languages and two cultures.

The stress and difficulties associated with adapting to city life in a new country are common to all the refugee families in La Playa who have to acquire not only a new language and new skills, but also a radically different perception of the world. This perceptual change is necessary in order for the Hmong to understand life from a new cultural perspective. Many circumstances influence Hmong families' ability to cope with the change in values, the new experiences, and the pace of acculturation. Undoubtedly the school plays a key role in the socialization of Hmong families to an American lifestyle and English literacy. The authors saw some families surviving crises and adapting quite well; we saw them becoming wise with money, buying homes, and encouraging their children to continue with their education in community colleges. Some families, on the other hand, began to fall through the cracks in American society through neglect, prejudice or ignorance. Those families living on a fixed welfare budget, and unable to afford increasing rents, were forced to relocate once again, and experienced the trauma of repeatedly uprooting children and family. The effect of relocation on the family unit as a whole, as well as on individual family members, was severe and misunderstood by well-meaning outsiders.

Children, who were transitioning and adjusting rapidly to a new culture, internalized relocation stress and tried to find different strategies to cope with it. The family offered them varying amounts of support depending on the parents' level of English language proficiency and their level of sophistication in dealing with American society, as well as the amount of time they had to spend with their children. In the following parent's conversation, there was further insight into the dilemma of cultural conflict and to the confusion felt by the older generation. 'My son can't be American because he's Hmong. I don't know if he'll want to learn Hmong things. Maybe he doesn't know how to think — because when a cassette comes from Thailand and we turn it on to listen to it — he gets mad and goes, ''Turn it off!'' He doesn't want to hear it. In some ways he is stupid and doesn't know what is right' (Jacobs, 1986).

Children in School: Facing Teachers

Children are often unaware of the long-term implications of how changes in language and culture influence their self-perception of ability and self-confidence. They may lose their mother tongue before they can communicate fluently in the second language. As they try to adjust to school, while at the same time trying to maintain their attachment to home values, they often feel divided and unable to cope with demands from either school or home. Indeed, many children lose their self-esteem as they face daily embarrassing failures in school, but others succeed in integrating home and school values, in addition to performing well in academic tasks. As Hmong children went through school activities they began to internalize new values and the teachers' views of their own competence.

The four Hmong students discussed in this chapter (Chou, Son, Pao and Vang) were in two classrooms. Mrs. McCarthy, Chou and Song's teacher, had recently implemented cooperative learning strategies. Pao and Vang's teacher used a more teacher-directed large group teaching approach. We wanted to know what was peculiar about these children who succeeded, and what was the role of teachers and other personnel in fostering the success or contributing to the failure of those children.

These students' encounters in school became at times frustrating, and at worst traumatic, as they attempted to belong and participate fully in classroom learning activities. They became increasingly aware of their collective and individual cultural differences and values as seen through the eyes of their teachers and peers. Feeling unusually high levels of anxiety and stress, they sought alternatives to cope with classroom activities. Their teachers, although well meaning, remained securely attached to their own training and cultural values and demanded compliance with American cultural norms of performance, which they communicated to the children in the English language. When the teachers' expectations were not met, they passed judgments on the children's ability to learn and determined collectively with other resource staff that these children had learning disabilities. School personnel viewed these students as having low potential, performing at low levels of achievement, and giving clear signs of suffering learning disabilities, but neither teachers, nor principal nor psychologist could explain the nature of the presumed disability. The Hmong children under study showed deep frustration and an attitude of hopelessness as they failed to engage meaningfully in learning activities.

The school files often gave a very distorted picture of the students, and sometimes contained inaccurate information. A clear example of this was in the records of Pao. His kindergarten report contains the first mention of his mother's difficult labor, and the subsequent hospitalization of Pao in Thailand for dehydration and fever for the first two months of his life. Later, in Pao's written profile designed expressly to help the assessment team support a diagnosis of Pao's learning disability, his first grade teacher wrote, 'The kindergarten teacher told me his parents thought Pao was retarded so they never expected much from him at home.' In spite of the fact that this information was later proved incorrect, it functioned as a decisive influence on the school psychologist's assessment of Pao. Dr. Sandra White, the psychologist, referred to it in her report:

> It is of course exceptionally difficult to transcend cultural barriers and try to define the nature of a learning disability in a Hmong child. A remark in the cumulative folder is perhaps at least suggestive — on the kindergarten retention form there is a note to the effect that Pao's mother had a protracted labor and subsequent two month hospital stay after his delivery (Jacobs, 1987).

It is important to remember that parents reported the absence of translators at student conferences. Struggling in English, it is easy to see how things became confused. Later, with the help of a trusted translator, it was found out that the birth difficulties concerned Pao's brother — not him! Piecing together in retrospect the process of communication, it seemed that the typical comment of a Hmong parent about even an extremely bright child (*nws ruam ruam*, or literally, 'he is dumb') had been mistranslated originally as 'he is retarded'. Perhaps both Mrs. Vanderberg and Dr. White, were searching for a rationale to classify Pao. Questioned as to whether Pao's problems might be culturally based rather than a disability, the teacher replied, 'I think it is both . . . but probably heavier on the cultural side. Of course, it is true, some of the other children, from the same type of background, have done much better. So that tells me it must be some sort of learning disability' (Jacobs, 1987).

When the teacher claimed that Pao was from the 'same type of background' as others, she was only referring to the ethnic background and refugee status of the children. As we have previously discussed, it is apparent that family backgrounds and situations were very diverse. The questions we needed to ask were:

1. What information do the teacher and psychologist have to make the judgment that Pao has a learning disability?
2. What is the nature of the presumed disability?
3. Is this disability a permanent state, or a temporary condition during Pao's adjustment to American school and society?
4. Was it created by the school experience, by other factors extrinsic to the child, or is it an attribute of the child?

Classroom Participation

All the students exhibited more problems in their home classrooms than in the special classes (ESL, special education, etc.) even though the classrooms were bright and cheerful, and the teachers very sincere. The ratio of students to teacher, the use of English for instruction and the emphasis placed on individual work proved difficult for all four students. Both rooms had students arranged in clusters, and at different times during the day they were allowed to collaborate on work. Nevertheless, the children who were alienated from the teacher and classroom activities remained so, even though they were somewhat involved in interaction with classmates. Both Ms. McCarthy and Mrs. Vanderberg divided students into reading groups on the basis of skill level, and spelling was also done in these groups. Mrs. Vanderberg provided more instruction that took place in the large group, usually with individual work assigned, while Ms. McCarthy was experimenting with cooperative learning structures for math and some other assignments. Ms. McCarthy observed the following:

> At first I was hesitant to use it [cooperative learning] because the language specialist told us that our seating arrangement had to be such that the students were facing the teacher at all times, so that the students are always focused on you as the language model. But I decided to try it, and now we use it all day. It is so wonderful because the kids learn from each other, and they truly are helping each other. They truly care ... The motivation is incredible (Jacobs, 1987).

The cooperative clusters for the reading groups worked well, but not as smoothly for math, because some of the students seemed to resent the slower students. There was also conflict with group decisions. One time each cluster was deciding how to spend money earned at the school fair. An Anglo girl was strongly advocating the idea of buying ice cream. When a

Hmong girl refused to agree, the blond girl turned to her and said sarcastically, 'Do you even know what a banana split is?'

Both classroom teachers were dedicated women with a professed feeling of empathy for English as a Second Language (ESL) students. Mrs. Vanderberg expressed genuine concern over Pao, her lowest achieving student, and she repeatedly stressed that she knew he worked best in small groups. What stopped her from giving Pao special help were her belief that it was 'not realistic', since next semester he would need to function as one of the class. She elaborated further on what catastrophic events could result if extra help were given to Pao, or to other students like him. They would become 'unprepared' for their future work. Her conceptual framework did not include the idea that individualized attention for a while might help Pao become prepared to work on his own.

This belief system was apparent in other conversations with her as well. She mentioned that she knew Pao would do better sitting in the front of the class, but she moved him to the back after some time. 'I can't always keep him in the front, it isn't fair to the other children. And it isn't realistic, he can't always sit in the front' (Jacobs, 1987). The second class teacher was more willing to give help, but she too was caught up in the paradigm that it was 'unrealistic'.

In both classes, the teacher's aides were middle-aged Anglo women who had no special training in teaching. Although their job was to work with under-achieving students, and that included many ESL students at this school, they had not received training in crosscultural awareness or teaching methods. One of the aides was always quick to point out what the students could not do, and she did not seem aware of their competencies.

Near the end of the semester, student teachers took over the classes. They noted that their credential program had not prepared them for the special needs of a culturally diverse class, like the ones in which they found themselves. Furthermore, the La Playa school had not provided any in-services for the student teachers on this issue; they had only received a mimeo sheet about refugee children, with outdated and incorrect information.

One student teacher assigned a story for the lowest reading group to read that was about a Navajo boy who lived in 'two worlds', that of the reservation and that of town. During the discussion that followed, the student teacher tried to identify the nationality of each child in the group, sometimes confusing nationality with ethnicity. To the Hmong children she said, 'You're Laotian', to the Anglos she said, 'You're American', and to the Latino students she said, 'You're Mexican'. There was an awkward silence since it showed her ignorance of the distinction of Hmong and

Laotian ethnicity, and also offended some Mexican-American and Indochinese students who thought of themselves as American.

The four students responded to the stress of the expectations placed on them in their classrooms in different ways. Pao, a thin boy with angular features, showed facial expressions indicating emotional extremes — he was either sullen and withdrawn, or smiling and giggling. His happy face was only seen on the playground when he was engaged in physical activity with other Hmong children and was speaking in Hmong. In fact, his face was almost always down on his desk and covered by his arms when the teacher was speaking to the whole class. He was so disengaged that he would not even look at the teacher when she addressed the class as a whole. He began by listening, but within moments he either had his head in his arms, resting on the desk, or was doodling. He yawned constantly and seemed either tired or bored. The only time he participated was when the class reached a high energy level with everyone waving their hands; then he, too, raised his hand, but would quickly lower it when the teacher looked his way.

Often Pao drew while the class worked on assignments, and he did not respond to directions given to the class as a whole. He would not, for example, take out a book, look at the board, check work, or put away papers following the teacher's orders. If the teacher or his friend told him to do so directly, he would respond, but often did not remain on the task. When he did complete an assignment, he usually rushed through it, not checking it over. His main goal seemed to be completion, so he could draw. Interestingly, although Pao enjoyed drawing, during art class he was not an enthusiastic participant.

Song, a 9-year-old girl in the second class, had an opposite mode of coping. She is a tiny, extremely shy girl who was born in Laos and made the escape journey to Thailand. Her speech was always in a whisper, and her arms encircled her work, so no one else could see it, as she repeatedly erased what she wrote. Her concern over mistakes made her the slowest worker in the class. Her papers suffered at the hand of her over-erasing — holes appeared where the paper was worn away, and she usually ended up with just a couple of sentences written.

Song was a very serious student, and she always paid attention and tried to do all her assignments. In her own cooperative group of four students, there were two other Hmong children and one Chicano, and Song seemed to be at ease interchanging ideas with them. In other situations, where Anglo children were part of the group, she did not contribute as much and appeared meeker. When called upon to participate or share information with the whole class, she became shy, spoke in a whisper, and obviously was struggling. Song went beyond her personal shyness, though, for the sake of the group. This fit into her home values which stressed group cooperation.

The other two boys we observed during a reading lesson did some work and directed their energies to something more fun, like drawing, cutting and pas̲̲̲̲̲̲̲̲̲̲̲̲̲̲̲̲̲̲ thers. They rarely paid attention to the teac̲̲̲̲̲̲̲̲̲̲̲̲̲̲̲̲ remely talented in art; his work was admire̲̲̲̲̲̲̲̲̲̲̲̲

[handwritten: Untrained teachers who do not recognize what the student's interest]

Mrs. Va̲̲̲̲̲̲̲̲̲̲̲̲̲̲̲̲̲̲̲̲̲̲̲̲̲̲ journals that were not read by the teacher.̲̲̲̲̲̲̲̲̲̲̲̲̲̲̲̲ was the only assignment in which he became totally engaged. His ability to express himself in words varied drastically according to the context of the writing task. For class assignments he watched his spelling and punctuation, but produced very little text. Pao resisted writing themes that the teacher assigned and in this context his work showed no creativity or enthusiasm. On the other hand, his journal writing didn't concentrate on form, but rather on description of events. The entries illustrated his ability to write a complex story:

> Yesterday I went to the store with my mother and father and my little brother and my sister too. I saw a gobot [a toy that changes from a robot to a car]. Then I asked my mother. Then my mother said yes you may have that gobot. Then I pick it. I got some cookies too. Then we went to pae maney. When we got home I play with that gobot. And I have fun. Then i brot that gobot outside to play but a boy came out and then he said let me play with that gobot. Then I said no. Then he got a stik. Then he hit it. Then it was brokein. Then my mother said she will go and buy another for me. Then we went to the store and buy an other gobot for me. Then I play with that new gobot outside agone but when the boy came I ran insid. When he go inside Then I come out (Pao's journal entry, 5/8/86, from Jacobs, 1987).

The literacy and social skills evident in the journal entry were missing in the writing assignments for class. Following is a typical sample of Pao's work in response to an assignment. Mrs. Vanderberg told the class to write a story about a picture she gave them, and this is what Pao wrote:

On march i went outside to fly my kite. The wind was strong. It blew the kite [?]. Then it went down (Class Assignment, 5/5/86, from Jacobs, 1987).

A study of Pao's writing revealed that when he found a task to be meaningful, he was motivated to participate in writing assignments, and he was capable of displaying a skill level much higher than in other class situations. Mrs. Vanderberg was unaware of this, and expressed surprise when told that Pao had written long complex passages in his journal.

None of the four students claimed to be too happy in school. Pao's body language eloquently showed his attitude toward school; in the classroom his body was always positioned away from the teacher, limp, with his eyes downcast. In an interview this is what Pao said about school:

I: Do you like school?
P: Not very much.
I: What don't you like about it?
P: It's too hard.
I: I saw you do multiplication yesterday, remember?
P: It's too hard. I just guessed.
I: Sometimes when I look at you in school you look really unhappy.
P: It's too hard.
I: When you get to something hard, do you try? Or do you not do it?
P: Try. If I don't get it, I just guess. (Jacobs, 1987)

Although there are cultural impediments to a conversation of this sort which calls upon a child to express critical feelings about school, the responses indicate Pao's fundamental feelings about school. The dialogue revealed his unhappiness in the classroom, his feelings of inadequacy ('it's too hard' — repeatedly), and his feelings of powerlessness in obtaining the information necessary to learn what he doesn't know ('I just guess').

Although Song claimed to like school, she worried greatly about certain things. She revealed her deep fear of getting her name on the board (the teacher writes the names of misbehaving children on the board) or getting a ticket for bad behavior on the playground. Song also disclosed that she worried about giving a wrong answer when the teacher called on her. This is indicative of how Song experienced stress at school, not necessarily based on realistic possibilities. Her behavior did not make her a likely candidate for tickets or getting her name on the board. Her preoccupation with getting a wrong answer limited her ability to take risks in learning. The image of Song with hands encircling her paper to protect any mistakes from the eyes of others, and constantly erasing, exemplifies her mental state of anxiety and fear.

Song's teacher suspected that Song's problem was language, not an actual problem of ability. Nevertheless, she planned to refer her for placement in the disability program, since reading lab would be unavailable to her as a fourth grader. This illustrates the bind in which teachers find themselves. In order to get students small-group help, they need to be in the special education program.

Pao, Chou, Song and Vang were in the lowest reading groups in their classes. The other students in these groups were also minority students. Observations revealed that they spent little time actually reading, in fact, much less than the other reading groups. Their group was also the only group that did not have their reading assignments written on the chalkboard. Most of their group instruction time was spent in spelling and workbook activities supervised by the aide. Mrs. Vanderberg's explanation for this was that they needed pre-reading work to prepare them for reading. Because they spent less time reading, they worked more frequently with the classroom aide than with the teacher. Aides were not allowed to do any reading with the students, but were permitted to oversee spelling and workbook activities.

In Mrs. Vanderberg's class the reading group worked at a table near the side wall of the room. The aide sometimes sat at the head of the table, and sometimes stood behind the chairs of the students. She was a large woman, and when she stood behind the children sitting in their tiny school chairs, she appeared overpowering. She would often give directions and then send the students to their seats to do individual work. The aide usually had to repeat the directions for Pao, which upset her every time.

When the group actually read from a book, they worked with the classroom teacher, sitting in a half circle. The book they used was a first grade reader. In small group situations. Pao paid close attention. Commenting on this, the teacher said, 'In small groups it is better, but given the ratio of students to teachers, it's not realistic and each year he falls more behind.' Another time, discussing the same matter, the teacher stated, 'He [Pao] responds to adults if they are really on, but that's unrealistic, you can't always be on . . . ' (Jacobs, 1987). Again and again, there were situations in which the class teacher showed herself to be competent in drawing Pao into the group, but she invalidated the worth of this method by calling it unrealistic. The aide who worked with him every day did not have the skill to involve him. Unfortunately, the classroom aides did not have in-service from resource specialists, so they did not have information that might have enhanced their skills.

Pao often expressed negative feelings about this time in reading group with the aide. Frequently he said, 'Oh no, not again', when he was told to go to work with her. Once in the group he would often ask the aide, 'Can I go now?' Often, Pao's actions were misinterpreted by the aide. He talked aloud while he worked, for example he would say, 'This is hard', or, 'I got this right', but the aide did not use this as an opportunity to communicate with him. She saw it as talking ou⟨...⟩rn, rather than an attempt at initiating interaction. Other time⟨...⟩reted his blank look as an indication of a lack of knowled⟨...⟩ognizing it as possible passive resistance.

In her reading group, S⟨...⟩extention of the caretaking role she had at ⟨...⟩ents in this group who had a harder time th⟨...⟩ble for giving them assistance. This feeling ⟨...⟩ess, and consequently she was a more acti⟨...⟩of how Song became involved with the role o⟨...⟩d in her willingness to go against the rules in order t⟨...⟩A Hmong boy was having trouble completing an exercise⟨...⟩paper alligator. When Song finished her own, she made one for ⟨...⟩nd he handed it in as his own.

Ms. McCarthy, the teacher, expressed that she saw comprehension as Song's main problem in reading. The example she gave clearly shows the extent of cultural bias and misunderstandings. 'For example, the other day we were reading that story. It was obvious, too, but she [Song] didn't see that the child was worried about having stolen the book. The problem to her was that the girl had a nightmare, because that's I guess what she can identify with' (Jacobs, 1987).

Although McCarthy gave an indication that she understood that Song identified with a different problem in the story, her judgment told her that Song's problem was a 'lack of comprehension'. Obviously, the implications of nightmares in Song's culture, as well as from her own experience, were more problematic than stealing a book. Nightmares had serious meaning in Song's life, they could indicate unresolved trauma from the escape journey or bad spirits at work. From this perspective, Song was not having comprehension difficulties, but rather expressing her point of view.

Reading Lab

Song and Chou met with the reading specialist, Mrs. Willis, daily for twenty minutes in a separate classroom. The reading lab curriculum had *unfamiliarity with culture* [handwritten note on obscuring paper]

been designed to suppl████████████████ork. The skills taught included syllabi████████████████strategies, and comprehension. Students t████████████████s. Willis made a continuing diagram on the████████████████story map. The students discussed the class████████████ey read, as well as the characters, the setting████████████led higher level vocabulary words, which t██████████████ learned to decipher by context. While they read, she continuously checked to see if they understood the words they were reading.

The emotional environment of the class was very supportive. Mrs. Willis gave students time to think without being rushed by others who knew the answer. As an alternative to reading stories, they played games involving identifying sounds and making words. Right- and left-brain learning theory played an important part in the teacher's perspective of how children learned. She believed that children from different cultures used different sides of the brain for language centers. According to her, for example, some languages are pictorial and use the right-brain, while English is very left-brain. Because of this belief, Mrs. Willis felt that children from different backgrounds possibly needed different learning strategies than those used in the regular classroom.

Song exhibited the same anxious attentiveness in Mrs. Willis' class that she did in the rest of school. Although Song commented that she liked the class, she also noted that she was afraid of making mistakes. The small group might be a bit less stressful, but she worked best in cooperative rather than individualized situations.

Chou said that he liked reading lab better than his reading group, because Mrs. Willis helped him more. He participated fully in this class since its small size enabled her to keep him focused, and she encouraged him to pay attention. She also gave him plenty of positive reinforcement, and he responded well to her praise. At the beginning of the school year Chou was reading at the mid-first grade level. By June he was reading at the end of second grade, an improvement of one-and-a-half years in only eight months time. This rapid improvement illustrated that Chou made slow progress up to a point, and then he advanced quickly when he had acquired enough language background. The reading specialist saw Chou as a bright child, but agreed with his teacher that his immature behavior might require him to be referred for special education, even though intellectually he was capable of doing the class work.

Special Education Classes

Pao and the other Hmong boy went to a resource class for children with 'learning disabilities' every day for twenty minutes. Four other boys were in the room at the same time, but they worked either alone or in pairs with the resource teacher or the resource aide. It was a small, cheerful room with a handwritten sign that read, 'You can lead a horse to water and if he is thirsty, he will drink because it is a natural and pleasant thing to do.' This typified the philosophy of Mrs. Smith, the learning resource teacher. She was an older woman who was enthusiastic, but sometimes a bit patronizing. She felt all her students had actual disabilities, but that many of their difficulties were compounded by cultural differences, language problems, and post-traumatic psychological problems.

The resource class aide was hired for her bilingual Spanish/English skills. Unfortunately, she had no training in special education, nor was she familiar with the Indochinese culture. As the other classroom aides, she lacked skills with such techniques as positive reinforcement, building self-esteem, and motivational interventions. When the aide worked with students she appeared bored. She corrected mistakes but never offered explanations or checked for understanding.

Pao behaved differently in the resource class compared to how he acted in the classroom or reading group. His enthusiasm was apparent even in the buoyant way he walked to the class. Mrs. Willis did not criticize the students and created an atmosphere that encouraged the children to do their best. She responded to the students as if they were interesting people, which brought out these qualities in the students. In this situation Pao was responsive and self-assured. Consequently, Mrs. Willis had a different perspective of him than Mrs. Vanderberg, his classroom teacher.

The small size of the group permitted the teacher personal involvement with each student. This close contact enabled her to get to know Pao and the other boy as people; thus she was able to find out what was hard for them and what kind of help they needed. Mrs. Willis made certain that the readings were relevant to the lives of her students. For example, when they read 'Johnny Appleseed', she emphasized that Hmong people were pioneers as he was. In this class, the writing assignments were also fitted to the lives of the students. They wrote books about their family history, their likes and dislikes, their families, and their friends. Pao gave these assignments the same quality attention that he gave his journal writings. Both students responded with more energy, concentration, and greater skill than they had shown in any other situation. Their greater competence in this class appeared to be in direct relationship

[handwritten note: Tuning out things when powerless to bridge gap]

n in the classroom. A lot of it I do think is expectation — because I see so many foreign students just tuning out. Probably just from exhaustion.... In the bigger classroom he sees the other children getting it, and he is discouraged right away.... I am sure that when he is in his classroom, he just tunes out. The more that he takes the stance that it's too hard and he doesn't like it, the more he tunes out (Jacobs, 1987).

Pao displayed his non-participatory behavior in the resource lab when he worked with the aide. One day Pao was having trouble reading a story about a carnival. The aide became incredulous when Pao asked what a ferris wheel was and said that he had never been to a fair. Another time the story was about a boy going camping, and the aide asked Pao what he would bring with him if he were to go. Pao said he would take a gun, and the aide, obviously unhappy with the answer, asked 'Why?' Pao replied, 'In case there are robbers.' The aide was visibly disturbed and reprimanded him saying, 'There wouldn't be robbers.' She was speaking from her own experience, without realizing that in Pao's background he had heard stories of journeys from Laos to Thailand that included accounts of robberies and murders. Pao did not argue with her, he just tuned her out, just as he did in class when he felt powerless to bridge the gap between cultures.

Nevertheless, in the resource class Pao generally worked with Mrs. Willis, did his work, asked for help, offered suggestions, and smiled. In an interview, after Pao stated that he hated school, he was asked if he also hated resource lab. His response clearly showed why he preferred the latter:

P: It's better... it's easier.
I: So when you can do the work, you like school?
P: Yeah.
I: And in resource class, you can do the work.
P: Yeah.

Mrs. Willis mentioned that refugee children showed more progress in their work than their American counterparts. That is, American children with learning disabilities do not increase their learning skills at the pace of the Hmong children. It is very likely that Hmong children have been misclassified as 'learning disabled' because of their English language problems. Therefore, as Hmong children acquire English as a second language and become more familiar with the American culture, they improve their academic performance. Of course, the question is whether diagnosis of learning disability has been appropriate.

Concluding Remarks

Alienation from the social organization of the classroom decreases students' participation in academic activities and students' opportunities to learn, thus leading to a much poorer performance over time. Systematic observations of school personnel behavior raise a number of questions:

1. Under what circumstances do children participate actively in classroom activities?
2. What is their degree of ability in performing academic tasks which they find meaningful?
3. How can children be encouraged to transfer their communicative skills from their mother tongue to English?
4. Beyond the problem of knowing the English language and the school culture, what seems to prevent children from communicating effectively with teachers, English-speaking peers, and other personnel?

At the heart of participation structures in learning processes is the required comprehension of the nature of the task, its purpose, its instrumental value to accomplish certain goals, and the procedural steps to be followed.

It is also important to note that the cultural conflict between the teacher's values and the child's needs results in children being prevented from developing a personal bond with their teachers. Other studies (Trueba, 1989) suggest that achievement motivation in culturally different children is linked to the opportunity to develop a personal relationship with adults or knowledgeable peers who help children in attacking cognitive tasks which are seemingly decontextualized and meaningless. The dialogue between Pao and his teacher poignantly spoke of his growing alienation from school.

T: Will you miss La Playa School?
P: No, I hate.
T: Did you hate school last year too?

P: Sort of.
T: Do you hate it more this year?
P: Yes.
T: Why?
P: Because it's getting harder and harder.

A recurring theme emerged concerning the teachers who felt that they were in a double bind. The teachers were aware that these students worked best in a one-to-one or small group situation. After third grade, in order to get additional small-group learning time for students who were having difficulties keeping up with the class, the only resource available was the learning disability program. A well-meaning teacher, who felt that he or she could not give a student enough attention, would usually opt for labeling the child learning disabled in order to get them additional assistance.

Chapter five

Seven 'Learning Disabled' Indochinese: Institutional Approach to Children Facing Culture Conflict

Hmong children in school are one of several minority groups undergoing rapid sociocultural change as they make efforts to acquire a new language and culture. What the Hmong have in common with other Indochinese children is a non-Western culture and language, and the experience of the school culture. This brief comparative study focuses on how the school deals with Indochinese children facing learning problems related to their lack of familiarity with English and the American culture.

The impact of school on minority, immigrant and refugee children undergoing a critical period of pervasive changes in their lives is the focus of this chapter. How does the school handle children with learning problems? How do school personnel distinguish learning problems stemming from individual personality or physical handicaps from problems derived from cultural conflict and psychological stress related to culture shock and culture change?

Theoretical and Practical Significance of the Study

A comparison of seven Indochinese students, three Hmong, three Laotian and one Vietnamese, is presented here. These children were identified by school personnel as 'the most needy learning disabled' among forty-two children classified as 'learning disabled'. Why and how were the forty-two children (which is 7% of the total student population in the school) selected as 'the most needy learning disabled'? One of the most important criteria for the selection was the relative inability of these children to handle communication in English, especially reading and writing. In other words, English literacy has become a criterion in designating learning disabilities of newcomers to school.

The value of English literacy for Indochinese students — and for all immigrant and refugee students — is undeniable; it goes far beyond the school rewards of academic achievement and cognitive development. It profoundly affects their self-concept, their overall psychological adjustment, and their chances for future employment in the new society. The question is whether early classification as 'learning disabled' on the basis of deficiencies in English literacy is a legitimate criterion to identify culturally different children in need of special assistance.

One of the problems in the acquisition of English literacy is the subtle cultural conflict that involves teachers and children in the organization of classroom activities. There are different expectations and interpretations of what happens on the part of teachers and children, and gradually children find themselves classified as low-achievers. The resulting incidents of daily academic failure become a traumatic experience with devastating results. The seven Indochinese children under study were diagnosed as 'learning disabled' through a process of informal consultation between teachers and the school psychologist. This process, as well as the statements on the nature of their presumed disability, reflects a profound confusion on the part of the school personnel in dealing with children who do not share the same values, same language, and who consequently respond to school situations with unexpected behavioral patterns.

This confusion results from presumptions of academic competence, or lack of it, made by school personnel on the basis of acceptable linguistic and cultural responses (phonetically clear English utterances and kinetically familiar postures, gestures, eye contact, etc.). This is one of the manifestations of how cultural conflict affects both mainstream and minority populations. The interaction between minority students and school personnel is plagued by misunderstandings and misinterpretations on both sides. A number of questions of critical importance for schools in dealing with low achieving children are raised by this study:

- Is students' difficulty with English literacy a necessary and sufficient criterion for their classification as 'learning disabled'? (Rueda, 1987).
- Are some learning disabilities related to the school experience of minority children?
- Are some of these disabilities caused or increased, or simply neglected by mainstream schools?
- Is children's average performance in subjects requiring less English proficiency (for example, in math, science or art) proof of children's normal capacity?
- If part of the problem of minority underachievement is cultural conflict, what is the nature of this conflict, and how does it affect children's adjustment and their ability to learn?

- How does the experience of academic failure affect their self-esteem and their overall commitment to learn and succeed in America?
- What is, for example, the impact of the English-Only instructional policy on the Indochinese students?
- Specifically, did the English-Only instructional policy increase stress and trauma levels in some students to the point of jeopardizing their participation in academic and social activities as well as their overall development?
- Did this policy hinder the transfer of cognitive skills and slow the acquisition of English literacy?
- Did this policy lead to their social and psychological isolation, thus hindering their overall long-term cultural adjustment and academic success?

These and many other questions were constant reminders to researchers that we were dealing with very complex issues in cross-cultural research.

Teachers and school administrators who have control of the school make decisions affecting children's lives and their ability to cope with cultural change. School personnel, rather than generating new responses to the problems of communicating with Indochinese children, react with culturally-structured responses. This is precisely what makes both school personnel and children equal participants in the cultural conflict. Thus, behind some literacy and discipline problems there may well be serious and unresolved teachers' and students' misinterpretations of each other's behavior. Children's transition from the home to the school culture is as difficult as teachers' attempts to cope with the demands of a new student population whose language and culture are unknown (Spindler, 1974, 1982; Spindler and Spindler, 1983, 1987a, 1987b, 1989). And yet, illiteracy in English continues to be the most frequently recorded reason for classifying minority children as 'learning disabled'.

However, if we start with the assumption that in general all Indochinese (and other minority) children are competent enough to handle difficult learning tasks in the home and out-of-school settings, including the acquisition of their language and culture, then we are pressed to search for more rational explanations that lead to individual attributes of deficiencies such as 'learning disabilities'. We must also assume that the acquisition of English literacy is not an intrinsically difficult task, but it becomes difficult in the social and cultural context in which children are expected to obtain it. Because English literacy will continue to affect the future educational level and socioeconomic status of large numbers of minority students, it is important to explore ways of optimizing the sociocultural context of English literacy acquisition (Trueba, 1987a, 1987c, 1988a, 1988b, 1988c, 1989).

The Comparative Study

Since 1982 La Playa Elementary School has been the focus of a series of modest ethnographic research studies, including several doctoral dissertations and field projects. More recently, however, special efforts have been made to study systematically Indochinese students (Vietnamese, Hmong, Laotian) who are a significant part of the minority student population accounting for 40% of the total school population.

The study was conducted via systematic observations, interviews, tape recordings and ethnographic analysis conducted over eighteen months (September 1984 to March 1986), along the lines of the work done by other educational anthropologists such as Mohatt and Erickson (1981), Au and Jordan (1981), Moll (1986), Moll and Diaz (1987), Trueba (1983, 1987a, 1987b, 1988c, 1989) and Spindler (1987a, 1987b).

As we mentioned in a previous chapter, the school which has twenty-five different linguistic groups may seem, and is, unusual in many respects. The school, however, with its ethnic and linguistic diversity brings into perspective important issues related to the role of language in the overall adjustment and successful schooling of refugee and immigrant children.

The recommendations of teachers and principal and the examination of student files resulted in the identification of forty-two students classified as 'learning disabled'. At the request of the teachers and principal, twelve were specifically selected for a more intensive study. From those twelve, seven were the Indochinese children discussed in this chapter. All seven had already been referred to, and tested by, the school psychologist and officially declared by her as 'learning disabled' on the grounds that they were having serious adjustment or achievement problems diagnosed through psychological tests and confirmed by teacher testimonies.

At this point the researchers' task was to observe and interview the seven students, to get as much information as possible about them from the principal, teachers and students' families. The assumption was that all seven children were facing a comparable degree of difficulty in school (see Table 5.1).

These children shared the common stigma of being Indochinese refugees, often perceived as 'strange', unable to speak English fluently, and the lowest achieving of their ethnic groups. Their English was extremely

Table 5.1 Subsample of Indochinese Refugees Classified as 'Learning Disabled' at La Playa

LAOTIAN	M	Dinar 3-20-73 (?) Laos	4	86*	Came to U.S. 9-15-82. Large family, angry, poor reader, UNHAPPY. Low performance and self-concept. Cognitive skills deteriorated.
	F	Arath 2-21-79 Laos	1	—	Sister of Dinar. Artistic talent. Physical disability? Complications at birth. Father was in prison, mother under stress, poor. Slow English development.
	F	Ouan 12-4-73 (?) Laos	5	92*	Slow progress. Quiet. Paralyzed with fear in large groups. Reading comprehension 2.5. Tries hard. Health problems.
HMONG	M	Mou 7-18-76 Thailand	3	104*	Retained in Kindergarten. Reading level 1.8. Oral fluency in English. Unmotivated, distracted! Thought by teachers to be retarded!
	M	Tao 6-21-75 Laos	3	87	Reading comprehension and auditory processing problem. In this country since 1970. Retained in Kindergarten.
	M	Tou 10-7-76 Thailand	3	111*	Bright. In the U.S. since 1980. Reading and writing problems in ESL class. Fluent bilingual English oral proficiency.
VIETNAMESE	M	Bou 11-27-77 Vietnam	2	—	Speaking difficulties. In the U.S. since 1984. Speech therapy. Problems with English syntax and vocabulary. Affectionate!

*(Verbal scores not included)

limited. Two of the Hmong children, Mou and Tow, had enough command of the language to carry on simple conversations outside of class, but sometimes could not follow directions, and had serious problems understanding the teacher's lessons.

Researchers felt that the study of participation patterns in instructional activities would show the degree of meaningful and active engagement of students' academic progress, their level of English literacy and their overall school adjustment. The analysis of text produced by students was also considered exceptionally important, especially comparing their writings over a period of time.

General Findings

The learning problems of the seven Indochinese students were manifested in the form of a general disengagement or disinterest in school activities, inadequate participation in class (especially in whole group activities), low academic productivity in comparison with their peers, in school and at home, and clear signs of intensive emotional stages of fear, anxiety and stress.

To illustrate some of the limited participation patterns observed, we will offer concrete examples below. In general, these patterns, which have been discussed elsewhere (Trueba, 1983), can be reduced to three types:

1. Hypo-participation, characterized by extraordinary efforts to become inconspicuous or uninvolved.
2. Hyper-participation, characterized by obsessive efforts to look engaged, though only superficially, imitating reading or writing behaviors without being able to process information.
3. Hostile participation, characterized by selective engagement in activities for the purpose of venting anger or other negative feelings experienced in the school context.

Ouan, an 11-year-old Laotian girl, reading at the second grade level, was placed in fifth grade. The ESL teacher warned us that Ouan rarely talks, and, 'When pushed, Ouan talked in some complete sentences but her expressive language is still very weak.' The fifth grade classroom teacher said, 'Her attitude and attentiveness are good. I felt she was trying, but don't really know, because I don't remember her speaking at all!' One morning, in a group of four minority children during the reading lesson, the teacher presented a list of words needed for the reading lesson: 'fuss, snooze, separate, rock garden, marigold, and zinnia'. The children were then asked to read silently the first paragraph. The teacher asked, 'Is there anybody who did not finish?' The teacher quickly read the passage and began to discuss vocabulary. Ouan avoided eye contact and persisted in keeping her eyes down. The teacher asked, 'Ouan, what is snooze?' Ouan did not move. After a very short pause, the teacher gave the right answer: 'Like when you take a nap, you know, a sleep.' The lesson went on like that, with Ouan stressed, continuously moving her feet and hands, and shaking all over. She looked terrified of being asked another question. Similar incidents took place as the teacher attempted to cover the other parts of the lesson. Naturally, she could not understand what was going on, and she was clearly frustrated. At the end, Ouan stood up without having said a single word, ran to the side of her Laotian girlfriend and whispered something to her in Laotian. The math lesson, with another teacher, showed similar interactional, but less stressful, patterns partially because the teacher knew it was better not to ask Ouan to answer aloud, in front of the other students. The teacher would approach Ouan's bench and ask her softly, 'Do you know how to divide these fractions?' Ouan would shake her head and the teacher would do the operation on Ouan's paper.

Dinar is a 12-year-old Laotian boy who — at the time of the study — had been in this country for two and a half years. He is sociable but has a volatile temper and moves his feet, hands and eyes constantly, in almost uncontrollable fashion. His restlessness increases with demands for public performance, for example, during reading lessons. The teacher no longer asks him to read a brief sentence, because she knows that he will refuse and kick the bench in anger. Dinar says he likes school, but not the main teacher or the English language. The teacher noted in her report that for Dinar 'even counting beans and trading for ten sticks is hard'. He has made little progress in math over the last year, and his friends say that he has older siblings who 'yell at him and hit him a lot'. His reading teacher wrote in the monthly report, 'Poor Dinar, he didn't have a clue . . . , but he tried so hard with the less difficult materials I gave him; it was sad . . . ' Then, in a slightly more positive tone, she goes on to note: 'Dinar is an excellent artist and has superior motor skills, but something is not attached right' (Trueba, 1985).

Outside the main class, in the Special Education or ESL small groups, Dinar seems to be more involved in doing academic work. His main class teacher's opinion is in contrast with that of the ESL teacher who finds him smart and willing to learn. From the field notes taken during the ESL classes, the following will give the reader a feeling for the type of learning environment created in small groups:

Dinar had great anxiety today about his homework assignment. He tries to read it and cannot understand it. The teacher keeps trying to explain. He is bored. Does not pay attention to directions any more. The teacher comes to talk to him, and he says, 'I want to be in Laos. No. I don't want to be anywhere.' Then he tells Richard (a child in the same class) 'fuck you', and gets into an argument (Trueba, 1985).

For a minute it looked as if Dinar was going to lose control of his temper:

His face is red and the veins are clearly protruding. He cannot talk out of anger. Goes out of class and comes back shortly. He apologizes to Richard, and says to the teacher, 'We're friends now.' Then he goes back to the theme 'I don't want to be here,' and adds 'I had many animals in Laos — ten horses and many chickens' (Trueba, 1985).

Observations of Dinar in the large classroom, however, show that he usually was restrained and tense. One day, during a movie on Vietnam shown by the teacher (perhaps with some degree of insensitivity to the children who had lived through the horrors of the war), he walked out very angry, saying loudly something nobody understood. There were similar instances of cultural insensitivity. On another occasion, the teacher was asking the children to write about their fears, 'Like being scared, with bombs,' she said. Many students, including Dinar, sat quietly looking at their papers, refusing to deal with such a demand.

Students' written compositions were an eloquent statement of the problems of dealing with literacy in a culture and society which is totally unknown. The compositions from Ouan show, at the same time, determination to succeed and extreme difficulty handling relatively simple concepts and linguistic forms. It shows the serious problems Ouan is facing in school handling academic work:

When I am 18 I plan to get an car I am going to ride to school I will learn more I think I would go to college or UCSB I will learn and if I learn college I will graduate. when I am 22 I will found a work to do or learn more english again or I will ask my brother to found me some work to do (Trueba, 1985).

While these students were struggling to produce or interpret text, they experienced deep frustration and hopelessness. In the interviews we conducted with them, the students described classroom activities and talks with the teacher as too fast and too difficult, and their homework as confusing and boring. They would sometimes sit, yawning and asking: 'Is it time to go?' (meaning to go home). Other times they would just smile, look around, get up and, if the teacher was looking at them, pretend to write or read. If asked how the task was progressing, they would say, 'I don't know what to do.' Ouan, however, would say nothing. She would often pick a book and copy from it words or sentences that were not part of the assignment, without understanding their meaning.

As she became increasingly more isolated during classroom time,

Ouan's performance deteriorated in two important ways as our study progressed:

1. Her compositions became more fragmented and less meaningful.
2. Her actual participation in school activities was less frequent.

She was left alone in the corner of the class. Her fear of performing in public became insurmountable. Towards the end of 1985, after much work, she wrote in almost illegible writing:

> Today I was drawing a cat picture. My firend [friend] told me to ware dress. I eat orange yesterday. My bother [brother] have [has] a big map. Yesterday my mother make a sandwish [sandwich]. Las night I call my firend [friend]. I was sit [sitting] on a big rock. Yesterday I see [saw] many star [stars] (Trueba, 1985).

In February of 1986, after two and one-half hours of hard work, Ouan wrote the following composition:

> At my house we have 13 people in the house and we have three bed room [bedroom] my brother my brothe [brother's] wife sleep in one bed room [bedroom] my brother have a lot of cloth and my bed room [bedroom] is environment [spacious] because we have 7 people in my bedroom and we have lot of cloth to and other bed room have 4 peope [people] sleep in my house is environment (Trueba, 1985).

In March of 1986, she started to write very short compositions and withdrew more from classroom activities. When asked why her work was shorter, during one of the interviews, Ouan said, 'Mrs. X [the math teacher] never speaks to me. I have lots of time with nothing to do.' She had been very quiet for several days. One day she came and said to the ESL teacher, 'I don't want to be nothing when I grow up . . . I loved my horses in Laos. We had a brown and a white one. Love my animals.' From that time to the end of the academic year, Ouan just sat, copied simple sentences and turned in assignments with the same errors, sometimes fifteen to twenty in a paper.

Dinar was clear and forceful in stating his unwillingness to be in America. He often said, 'I don't want to be here; I want to be in Laos.' Even when he tried to relate to American cultural traditions, he could hardly understand them. For example, he wrote the following composition on Halloween:

> I Buy A pumpkin and I Drow [draw] my punkin [pumpkin] face is gross: — One boy came and trick or treat at my hous [house] and the punkin [pumpkin] (is took) [?]. The boy ran and throw the candy and the punpkin [pumpkin] laugh. — The boy cry and go homes and tell his mother. Boy come [The boy came] trick or treat, can you give some candy and the pumpking said no and I will give the boy candy to you. They boy wan...[?] (Trueba, 1985).

Here is a Christmas story by Ouan:

> Christmas is come you get to get out the school 10 day [days] and you can play all they lomg [all day long]. And get preempts [presents]. You [Your] mother love you are [a] lot and she buy you a preemts [present] it [if] you is [are] a good boy [girl?] (Trueba, 1985).

In talking with these children, it became apparent that the content of many compositions and reading lessons, when focused on stories about holidays such as Halloween, July 4th, Thanksgiving and other cultural traditions, often became meaningless. The level of difficulty, however, was not as great as in the use of taxonomic structures, for example in compositions or lessons focused on the flora and fauna peculiar to the United States. This was the case of Dinar and Ouan, as well as of the three Hmong children. Many objects, and many taxonomic concepts about the organization of these objects, were culturally foreign to them.

Mou is a 9-year-old Hmong boy, whose father is literate and whose family is well respected by other Hmong in La Playa. Chou is alert and competent in school, but perceived by the teachers as unmotivated, somewhat confused about his background, his home culture and place in school. He is easily distracted, daydreaming and absorbed with the beautiful drawings he makes. He can draw wild animals, people, and landscapes. The detail and proportion of his drawings demonstrate exceptional skills. Our classroom observations indicate that he is uninvolved and not very concerned with school work, but he can achieve above average levels. He tells the teacher he forgot to do his homework, but tells us he stayed up late watching television.

To Tao and Tou the language of instruction, English, is extremely difficult, and their families do not have a literacy tradition in any language. Writing and reading are seen by their parents as something generated by the Americans for other Americans. To what extent this view is shared by Tao and Tou, is not clear, but the content of the textbooks could easily reinforce this attitude.

The study showed quantitative evidence of less academic productivity in classroom tasks and homework assignments on the part of the seven Indochinese children under study (in contrast with their peers). Also, the quality of the linguistic structure and penmanship was much lower, in comparison with mainstream children and with other minority high-achieving children. This fact, however, should be explained.

Contrary to teacher expectations, Mou and Tou several times surprised their main teachers with unexpected amounts of text produced during English as a Second Language or special education classes on subjects selected by students themselves. And even the least involved students from our sample, Ouan and Arath, would sometimes bring pages of text and lists of words literally copied from books, dictionaries and other sources without much regard for its meaning. When we asked them why they did that while they had not completed the mandated homework, the answer was that their parents made them do so. That exercise seemed to the researchers to be a rather mechanical exercise related to the physical production of text without processing it. But it was not an empty and purely mechanical one; it made them familiar with words which eventually appear in classroom exercises and textbooks; more importantly, it provided these children with some measure of credibility. They felt that indeed they also could produce pages. This was the case for Ouan, for example.

In general, the seven Indochinese students tended to be relatively passive during classroom activities and to produce homework or other text in a typically fragmented fashion, with grammatical problems of the type shown above. In many instances, the observer could find evidence that they were not grasping the central meaning, or at times even the intended purpose of the task. Worse still, sometimes there was no participation whatsoever. Mou, for example, would keep his head down on the bench the entire class period, and so would Trac and Arath, though less frequently. All seven children tended to exist in isolation; they just sat quietly, daydreaming as if they had entirely given up any attempts to make sense of the world around them. This was less frequently the case of Dinar or Ouan. There was one important exception to this lack of participation and lack of productivity. During small group sessions with tutors, or in English as a Second Language and special education sessions, children were encouraged individually to select the content of the task and were given assistance step by step. Dinar, Ouan and Tao produced imaginative text (albeit full of errors) describing experiences (real or fictitious) in their home countries.

From the long interviews with main classroom teachers, we realized that these teachers rarely saw the sample children as being actively involved in learning activities. One of the teachers commented about Dinar, 'Poor Dinar, he does not have a clue'. Another said about Bou and Arath, 'they are like little vegetables', and about Mou, Tao and Tou 'they are hopeless'. Other comments regarding these and other minority children very explicitly pointed at the presumed lower mental ability of these children, almost echoing the psychologist's written comments in the files.

From daily observations, the researchers have some evidence that the children were going from a state of deep depression and mental isolation to a state of panic, and back to isolation. This was shown in their decreasing attempts to participate, to respond to questions, or to focus on simple directions. Certain undefined fears or perhaps other anxieties were expressed in physical restlessness, unfocused changing gaze, uncontrolled movements of feet and hands, frequent trips to the bathroom, crying, temper tantrums and other signs of emotional turmoil. These manifestations of emotional turmoil seemed to increase when a child was called by the teacher to perform in front of the class. Sometimes children were unable to control their emotions and they had to run to the bathroom, or get out of class, feeling obviously upset or humiliated and mortified. Field notes indicate that such embarrassment was apparent in instances when the teacher asked specific questions about reading, math, or homework which children could not answer. When Ouan and Tou had to read in front of the class, they would get physically upset, and soon after they had to excuse themselves to go to the bathroom. Dinar would show his anger, with a strong 'I don't know' that would discourage the teacher from asking again. The teachers interpret this response as a challenge to their authority and a sign of disrespect.

Arath, Tou, and Bou are very shy and rarely talk with anybody about their problems in school. They appear to be embarrassed and confused when the teacher asks them any question in the main classroom. In contrast, during our experimental interventions in small group interaction during English and reading sessions, stress was minimized by allowing these children to select the areas and pace of activities, and the level of skill associated with each activity. All three were communicative. Some music, an informal learning environment and a consistently affectionate, personal approach brought wonderful results. Dinar was often uncommunicative in the main class, but more open in the small class. An example from field notes about Dinar:

The English as a Second Language teacher is trying to help Dinar with his multiplication tables. He is very resistant after the 2's. Physically backed his chair away. He couldn't look at the teacher. He had a great deal of trouble with the 3's and was embarrassed. The teacher talked about how important knowing multiplication tables is, and she offered to take as long as Dinar needed to study them. He said he could not come next week because he was going to die. They talked more outside and the teacher said smiling: 'Don't die; not just yet; we need to work together.' Dinar laughed, but he continued his great resistance (Trueba, 1985).

We observed Arath and Tao calling themselves, in contexts similar to the one above, 'I'm dumb, I'm dumb', and talking about killing themselves. I have mentioned above Dinar's anger when a Vietnamese movie was shown in his class and when he engaged in an argument during English class. I also mentioned how Ouan would rather remain quiet and resist passively when asked to answer questions about readings she did not understand. The same strategy was observed in Arath and Trac in reading classes which usually had materials unknown to them. Performing in another language, at a level of skill far above that yet reached, on areas and topics which required rather complex cultural knowledge, in the opinion of the participant observers, became a traumatic experience with detrimental psychological side effects.

We also saw children pretending to be unable to perform tasks they had already mastered in private or in a small group. A case in point was Oudin who, after he learned the multiplication tables, would refuse to answer by simply saying, 'I don't know'. Difficulties in the use of the English language during instructional activities had a seemingly cumulative demoralizing effect on the Indochinese children, to judge from the decreasing level of participation and productivity during written and oral assignments. The examples above of Dinar's and Ouan's compositions illustrate this statement.

Summary of Findings and Implications of the Study

The summary is organized into the following categories: children's ability level, school prejudicial environment, teachers' role, increasing deterioration of cognitive skills, the importance of language for cognitive development, and cultural insensitivity of school personnel.

Cultural Conflict and Adaptation

Children's General Academic Ability

A close look at the compositions presented earlier would suggest that these children had serious problems using the English language. They often could not distinguish semantic ranges in the use of words, syntax was incorrect (verb tenses, word order, and structural inconsistencies), and they could not articulate descriptions of incidents; most importantly, they could neither understand nor generate certain concepts (environment vs. spacious), taxonomic differences between types of flowers (zinnia vs. carnation), presents given and activities associated with diverse holidays (Christmas and Halloween), and other relationships expressed through text.

Their knowledge of the English language and/or the subject remained unclear, at the surface of the issues, and clearly inadequate to handle concepts and relationships associated with academic subjects. Their ability to communicate for academic purposes was much lower in comparison with that of their peers.

School Prejudicial Environment

Perhaps behind racial prejudice in La Playa it was not a clear racist philosophy, but rather a conflict in values and perceptions between school personnel and the Indochinese families. This is a conflict which can escalate to genuine xenophobia, the experience of anxiety about sharing physical space or interacting with people who exhibit unexpected behavior and unknown cultural, linguistic and physical characteristics.

School prejudice, however, can lead to isolation of ethnic children, who are themselves searching for appropriate emotional responses and interpretation of unexpected behavior from mainstream people. Teachers and principals adopt a rhetoric of educational liberalism and devotion to the democratic ideals of desegregation. In contrast, their actual attitudes and behavior are apparent under close classroom observation, in school reports, or in opinions expressed by teachers in interviews and group meetings. Many teachers find many minorities incompetent, and of limited academic potential, and are convinced that many are even disabled. Most of all, school personnel may have no concept of the nature and proportions of the cultural conflict that refugee and other minority children are experiencing in school. Teachers and the psychologist view intelligence as clearly measured by the IQ tests.

School personnel often view intelligence as the ability to score high in tests. Intelligence, from a broader interdisciplinary perspective, could be better perceived as the ability to pursue culturally-determined goals through activities deemed as instrumental in the achievement of such goals. These goals are viewed as enhancing cultural values that are collectively shared by the cultural group. Therefore, from this standpoint, mental ability is not primarily demonstrated by high performance levels on tests constructed by bearers of another culture, or by high performance in artificially constructed settings, but in natural social interactions. Intelligence in American society and culture is demonstrated in literacy tests because the American education system places high value on English literacy and test-taking. But IQ tests measure only a fragment of the individual's overall human capacity and skills, that is, those literacy-based skills needed for problem-solving situations through text in the narrow parameters of school subjects, not real-life ability to handle cognitive and social problems related to individual and collective survival. Thus the 'correct answers' in tests reflect degrees of assimilation of mainstream cultural values (neither universally accepted — across cultures and social classes — nor free of conflict with the values held by members of minority groups).

Role of Teachers

The primary role of teachers is not to manage classroom activities or discipline children in the classroom, but to guide, instruct, assist and inspire students in learning activities, and to inculcate the cultural values associated with learning. This role has been defined as 'assisting student performance' (Tharp and Gallimore, 1989), and it occurs very directly as teachers communicate with individual students and assist them in internalizing the process and the content of learning activities. Cognitive processes, such as the discovery of relationships between concepts, theoretical premises, and object categories on the basis of specific information provided by textbooks and teachers, require a clear understanding and internalization of cultural values and the ability to control language in order to establish those relationships.

Racial prejudice about the ability of Indochinese children in La Playa, whether conscious or unconscious, is deeply rooted in the misperception by mainstream teachers and peers that these children are academically incompetent because they have an inferior intelligence or an inferior culture, not because they have a different set of experiences leading to different values and cognitive system. Poor academic performance of

Indochinese children can also be related to problems in communication during the early stages of acculturation. Often initial failure, and the stereotyping that follows, can *create* learning disabilities in these students.

Children internalize their 'disability' as a personal negative attribute, because it is in these terms that mainstream persons see it. The concept of disability as applied to culturally different students is not defined in specific terms and with respect to specific domains of academic activities; it is viewed as a generalized, terminal condition of children. Indeed, at the present time, a learning disability can be a simple and temporary emotional or academic problem, a reading difficulty, or consistent low achievement in a subject associated with lack of interest in classroom activities. It can also be a serious psychological maladjustment requiring long-term professional counseling, such as a very serious psychological trauma followed by high level of stress, suicide attempt and general depression.

If cultural conflict lies at the heart of English literacy problems of Indochinese and other minority students, as our studies seem to indicate, and if minority students' initial adjustment problems can result in school-created disabilities, then we have the responsibility of finding ways to sensitize the educators to develop culturally congruent instructional models which are effective and non-damaging for minorities. In subtle and intangible ways cultural values affect students' ability to engage successfully in English literacy activities and interpret meaning from text. School experience and the acquisition of English literacy bring about changes in minority language and culture that create devastating conflicts, unless students are given the opportunity to integrate cultural values.

Deterioration of Cognitive Skills

The most disturbing finding in our research was that some Indochinese children have stopped trying to learn and have accepted and internalized their 'disabilities' as their own personal attribute, not as a consequence of historical circumstances and dysfunctional instructional arrangements.

Evidence of this fact were the self-deprecating statements made by Dinar and other Indochinese children, and the profound depression of Ouan and Mou. The overall decrease in participation in classroom activities and the documented deterioration of reading and writing skills show that some of these children did not see much hope of ever improving their performance. To confirm teachers' suspicion that children's 'disabilities' and academic failures were always a personal characteristic, the seven children were tested by the school psychologist (the 'expert' in the eyes of teachers and students) and all seven were officially declared 'handicapped', that is, special education cases. It did not matter that the testing took place in English, a language the children did not understand, or that the information leading to teacher referral was not accurate, or that the child's performance in domains such as art or mathematics was above average (Tou in third grade has a math score of 3.5; Mou is a recognized artist in the Hmong community).

English Language Development

One of the central issues raised by field-based studies with minorities is the need for a full control of the language of instruction, and the importance that precise, logical and sophisticated use of language has in effective classroom instruction and in the acquisition of literacy skills.

One of the main goals in the education of linguistic minorities is to help students acquire high levels of literacy so they can process information and develop their thinking skills. If some of the literacy problems faced by Indochinese children are related to their different experiences, cultural knowledge, values and overall background, could the use of their native languages facilitate their cultural adjustment and school achievement? The assumption (Cummins, 1986) is that the ability to structure knowledge and to approach learning tasks effectively can be best acquired through the native language and then easily transferred to a second language. Use of native language is best because critical thinking skills and cognitive structuring are conditioned by linguistic and cultural knowledge and experiences that children usually obtain in the home and bring with them to school (Cummins, 1986).

Cultural Insensitivity of School Personnel

Another important issue, linked to the first, is that the nature of literacy problems faced by Indochinese and other linguistic minorities is deeply related to their limited knowledge of American culture, and the wrong assumption of instructors and textbook publishers that the lack of cultural knowledge can be neglected.

There is a serious ignorance and pervasive insensitivity by school personnel and textbook writers regarding the inherent inaccessibility and confusion for minorities reading text written with mainstream middle-class American children in mind. Such insensitivity to the obvious cultural and linguistic gap between minority home cultures and mainstream cultures paves the way for school personnel to stereotype and underestimate minority children's learning potential.

Positive Attitude

Are we teaching Indochinese children to fail in school? Is research on linguistic minorities' academic failure accomplishing anything? It has indeed attracted more attention than research on their success. Gradually, criticisms of such an emphasis have modified the focus of the research to one of differential achievement across minorities and across all student populations (Ogbu, 1974, 1978, 1987a, 1987b; McDermott, 1987a, 1987b; Trueba, 1983, 1986, 1988b), and to an approach which pursues interventions to create success (Moll and Diaz, 1987; Trueba, 1987a, 1987b, 1988c, 1989). The liberal position of the earlier social scientists studying education (Bidwell and Friedkin, 1988), who had questioned the 'leveling' and 'democratization' impact of schooling in the United States, has been welcomed by the radical reformist, Neo-Marxist and liberal researchers who view success or failure more as a function of societal factors than of either school treatment or student characteristics. The focus on success is consistent with an overall recent trend in the social sciences to look into the school treatment as a complementary explanation for success or failure. Bidwell and Friedkin state:

> To take the US as a case in point, one would expect that after so many years of public and professional debate about equality of educational opportunity, American elementary and high school would have taken effective steps against ascriptive biases in educational opportunities and achievement. Instead, American common schools seemingly transmit these biases, strengthening them in the process (Bidwell and Friedkin, 1988: 467).

McDermott goes a step further in his implied criticism of social science research:

> There is a preoccupation among us: Because we claim to offer good education to all and because many minority people seem to reject it, we are plagued with the questions of 'What is with them anyway?' or 'What is their situation that school seems to go so badly?' Their situation! . . . The breakthrough comes when we

realize that their situation is not theirs alone; it is ours as well. We help to make failure possible by our successes...Failure is a culturally necessary part of the American scene. We do not need to explain. We need to confront it...; explaining it will only keep it at a distance, making us its slaves (McDermott, 1987b: 361–363).

Racial prejudice and conservative trends, such as the English-Only movement, reflect the political clouds that have obscured the discussion of fundamental pedagogical principles that are applicable to all children, especially to minority children. These principles must be clearly stated and applied, even if political pressure and racial prejudice become an obstacle. One is prompted to ask: What has historically been behind such strong political movements which attempt to curtail the use of non-English languages in educational and other public institutions? From the early 1880s, when Connecticut, Massachusetts, Rhode Island, New York, Wisconsin and other states declared English as the mandatory school language, to the late 1960s, when the Bilingual Education Act was approved, there have been important changes. Yet, the memory of jailing and subsequent trials for speaking other languages is still fresh in the memory of some minority persons, who are ambivalent about the instructional use of languages other than English.

Many mainstream Americans have felt in the past, and still feel, that this country cannot rapidly assimilate immigrants, refugees and other minorities in numbers as large as in the past, and they see minorities' presence as a real threat to national unity and economic progress. A sad example of this position appears in history from time to time; the period between 1880 and 1930 was characterized by legislation intended to curtail the voting rights and general participation of linguistic minorities in social, political and economic institutions. Likewise, the ongoing English-Only movement which began in California (in 1986) has now spread to many other states and repeats history.

To pursue effective instructional approaches, educators must first understand the actual home cultural background and previous experiences of Indochinese children. Education cannot design instructional interventions expected to open the door to academic success, without better understanding the social context, conditions for school failure, and the process itself of socialization for failure.

School children, particularly those who are going through rapid cultural change and are not achieving well in school, may need extra time and flexibility to place themselves in a new cultural setting. The interpretation of daily interactional experiences at home, school and community, as well as of their own thinking processes, requires time and support. The opportunity for peaceful reflection, and for the interpretation of traumatic experiences, can permit children to make the transition to the new culture and language with less pain. Children's adjustment to school is often impacted profoundly by the pre-arrival experiences they face, the loss and separation from relatives, the feeling of guilt associated with this loss and separation, as well as the many degrading and traumatic incidents (DeVos, 1973, 1984) experienced by many refugees and low-status immigrants. These experiences are often reinforced in school encounters and may easily lead to a profound anxiety about self-worth and personal safety.

There are certain antecedents which seem to lead to experiences of individual and collective failure and which result in additional stress, ultimately creating a cumulative sense of impotence, isolation and low self-esteem. Because the acquisition of academic knowledge, particularly towards the end of elementary school, requires a very sophisticated use of the instructional language, minorities are set up for failure, a failure which becomes devastating for some Indochinese children. Learning, viewed from the socially- and culturally-based perspective advanced by the sociohistorical school of psychology led by Vygotsky (see McDermott, 1987a, 1987b; Goldman and McDermott, 1987; Trueba and Delgado, 1988; Trueba, 1987a, 1987c, 1988a, 1988c, 1989), requires that the learner play an active role in determining the whats and hows of the learning process. Minority children, as shown in the study reported here, often find themselves cognitively isolated and lost.

The fact that instruction is in English and is not tailored to the children's cultural knowledge and refugee experiences (a societal or structural failure) is perhaps unavoidable, but still not the fault of the children. Learning to succeed in the school interactional context has a powerful effect for success in other contexts, and for personality integration, as well as the development of a positive self-concept.

School socialization of minority children for academic success requires the creation of culturally-congruent learning environments in which Indochinese children find opportunities to learn well, and in which academic failure and embarrassing incidents are practically impossible. This can be achieved by identifying children's experiences, domains of knowledge and learning skills that insure high levels of performance and involvement. Furthermore, classroom activities must have clear goals, well-understood and internalized by minority children, and fully supported by their families.

In the end the purpose of creating a culturally-congruent pedagogical environment is to break the vicious cycle of stress, poor performance, humiliation, depression and failure. Stress will be minimized by the joyful experience of success, and by providing assistance to minority students as they need it. Learning should become gratifying in itself, as well as a socially rewarding experience when it takes place in a climate of warm personal relationships.

The goal is for Indochinese students to become self-sufficient, and to internalize self-regulating mechanisms during difficult academic tasks. To this end, Indochinese students need to internalize new 'successful experiences' as attributes of their own person and as components of their self-image that permits each of them to take new risks and venture into new learning experiences.

Chapter six

Culture and Minority Achievement:
Implications for Research and Instructional Practice

The aim of science is to seek the simple explanation of complex facts. We are apt to fall into the error of thinking that the facts are simple, because simplicity is the goal of our quest. Seek simplicity and distrust it. (Alfred North Whitehead)

The role of educational research in helping the Hmong is clear. But we must design research that offers a long-term commitment to educational reform and genuine concern for helping minority people.

Action Research and Literacy

The conceptual and methodological approaches will have to be uniquely suited to creating new opportunities for improvement. Action-research, or intervention-research, or field-based applied research, must be re-examined and tailored to the needs of minority education. This kind of research must also provide educators with a better understanding of the role of culture in the process of literacy acquisition and mainstreaming.

The emotional and financial investment in the future, as well as other efforts that we must make in order to preserve democratic institutions and the American way of life, must be guided by wisdom and understanding of American democratic structures. One needs to understand the role of immigrants and refugees in American democracy and their contributions in keeping alive the American dream of freedom for all and respect for ethnic cultures.

There is no doubt in our minds that Hmong youngsters will demonstrate their outstanding accomplishments in a variety of scientific fields and in the arts; they will display the virtues of their ancestors in their persistence, stoic adherence to cultural values and loyalty. Their successful performance in schools (e.g. junior high mathematics in the Lompoc,

California, schools is already evidence of their rapid acculturation and willingness to participate fully in American society and to make a significant contribution to our democratic system (Trueba, 1989).

There is still a great deal to do in Hmong education. Many young adults are unemployed and disenfranchised. Many adults live a life of idle isolation which is comparable to their dark years in the refugee camps of Thailand. Hmong adults have not found avenues for demonstrating their full potential to contribute to American society, primarily because there has been very limited assistance given to them in their adaptation to American social and economic life. In fact, many elders have been deprived of their useful role in Hmong society as American values change the entire lifestyle of the younger Hmong generations, including their religious beliefs.

Ethnic and minority groups in American society are torn in their acculturation, as they choose between the values and norms of the home culture and those of the social class and mainstream American culture. This conflict is embedded in the relationship between social class and ethnic membership. Hmong families who have moved up the social ladder tend to increase their involvement with mainstream Americans at the expense of their traditional values, ceremonies, religion and ethnic membership. Hmong youth want to belong in middle-class America, rather than maintain their parents' lifestyle, language and culture. They see English literacy and school achievement as the main instruments for emancipation from the status of refugee and for incorporation into mainstream affluent American society. Indeed, most Hmong youth are beginning to realize that English literacy and schooling mean empowerment.

Literacy for Empowerment

According to Goodenough, culture 'is made up of the concepts, beliefs, and principles of action and organization' (1976: 5). However, as Frake points out, the problem is not 'to state what someone did but to specify the conditions under which it is culturally appropriate to anticipate that he, or persons occupying his role, will render an equivalent performance' (Frake, 1964: 112).

It follows, therefore, that a thorough understanding of a culture requires a 'theory of behavior' in particular social settings. In other words, cultural knowledge and cultural values are at the basis of reasoning, drawing inferences and interpreting meanings. There is an important distinction between cultural knowledge and cultural values in the acquisition of literacy skills. The task is to make sense of text as a message whose content takes meaning within the 'concepts, beliefs and principles of action' alluded to by Goodenough. For this understanding we must have knowledge of the codes of behavior (the cognitive dimensions of culture), but we must also share in the cultural values (the normative dimensions of culture) through written communication. In order to see the culture-specific cognitive and normative dimensions operating in the literacy activities of minority students, it is necessary to observe such literacy activities systematically and in the home environment as well as in constrained school settings (Delgado–Gaitan, 1989).

The role of culture and cultural conflict has become observable in the last decade of interdisciplinary approaches to minority achievement, (Cummins, 1986, 1989; Trueba, 1988a, 1988b, 1988c, 1989; Spindler and Spindler, 1989), especially to the study of literacy and its role in empowerment (Freire and Macedo, 1987; Delgado–Gaitan, 1989). In the dialogue between Freire and Macedo this issue is discussed at length. The latter states:

> The notion of emancipatory literacy suggests two dimensions of literacy. On the one hand, students have to become literate about their histories, experiences, and the culture of their immediate environments. On the other hand, they must also appropriate those codes and culture of the dominant spheres so they can transcend their own environments (Freire and Macedo, 1987: 47).

Freire does not want to emphasize the social and cultural aspects of literacy at the expense of the individual. Therefore, to the above statement, he replies:

> I think that consciousness is generated through the social practice in which we participate. But it also has an individual dimension. That is, my comprehension of the world, my dreams of the world, my judgement of the world — all of these are part of my individual practice; all speak of my presence in the world ... In the final analysis, consciousness is socially bred (Freire and Macedo, 1987: 47).

Macedo goes on to emphasize that cultural process is 'intimately related with social relations, especially with class relations and class formations' and that it 'involves power and helps to produce asymmetries in the abilities of individual and social groups to define and realize their needs' (Freire and Macedo, 1987: 51). Freire, on the other hand, sheds some light on the relationship between literacy, culture and education as follows:

> Literacy and education in general are cultural expressions. You cannot conduct literacy work outside the world of culture because education in itself is a dimension of culture... [C]ulture is a totality cut across by social classes (Freire and Macedo, 1987: 51–52).

The relationship between understanding how culture or social class creates social strata with differential access to literacy levels and to educational levels is at the heart of the empowerment movement. If knowledge is power, where and how should we explore the role of culture/class in minority literacy acquisition? What is the expected impact of such research? Can it affect instructional practice? Overwhelmed by such questions, researchers often opt for taking a neutral, detached and safe position as pure researchers. Some of them go so far as to reject action, or applied, research as unscientific. Fortunately, there are other researchers who continue to explore the relationship between theory and practice — between conceptual models resulting from intervention-oriented research and the actual implementation of educational and social reform. The rationale for these efforts is that social science can also be built from the study of behavior in response to interventions.

Basic vs. Applied Research

Recent work of anthropologists, sociologists and psychologists (for a review of this work see Trueba, 1987a, 1987c, 1988a, 1989, but especially 1988b: 273–274) suggests that intervention and explanatory research are complementary to each other. The false dichotomy between 'basic' and 'applied' research is viewed by them more as the result of socio-political and historical events than as the logical organization of research endeavors (Trueba, 1988b: 273–274). The need for solid theoretically-guided research and for the study of educational interventions in schools with concentrations of immigrant, refugee and minority students is urgent. Educators want to understand better the kinds of learning environments that maximize the academic achievement of these students. It is in the organization of learning environments that students learn to manipulate symbolic systems, to comprehend, analyze and store in memory large bodies of subject matter content. The study of learning environments, beyond the observations of behaviors, with an understanding of the wider political, sociological and cultural parameters of behavior, will help educators create educational programs in which minority students internalize the values required to succeed in school. The study of reading and writing activities, for example, may lead to more imaginative and culturally-congruent organization of literacy programs that have the support of the ethnic community and family.

Field-based research will lead to a better understanding of the 'cultural embeddedness', (the role of culture) in underachievement, dropout and alienation phenomena of minority students. It is in the study of learning environments that we begin to see how teachers' familiarity with the minority home language and culture can be highly instrumental in understanding and communication gaps between students (and family members) and school personnel. The culture of the school mirrors the local culture of mainstream school personnel as well as the larger culture. Both the school culture and the larger culture determine how immigrants and refugees are perceived, treated and valued. School cultural environments often do not reflect enough sensitivity or understanding of the ethnic cultures of minority students in the organization of classroom activities, and, consequently, do not capitalize on the home culture in order to maximize student participation in learning activities. For example, in order to engage minority children in reading activities and as a bridge to help them understand the school culture, the children can be encouraged to generate text materials based on their own experiences (Trueba, 1989b). Learning experiences in the home are not trivial; they prepare children in acquiring a concept of the world, in using inquiry strategies, building taxonomic knowledge, making logical inferences and interference resulting from cultural conflict (see studies by Delgado–Gaitan, 1987a, 1987b, 1989). The analysis of learning experiences in the home does provide insights into possible linkages between self-empowerment efforts on the part of minority families and the supportive role that school personnel can play.

The social sciences have begun to re-examine their priorities. Erickson, for example, called to our attention the need for interdisciplinary approaches to understand academic learning:

> Individual cognitive functioning has been largely the purview of cognitive psychologists who have often attempted to study thinking apart from the naturally occurring social and cultural circumstances. The anthropology of education often has studied *anything but* deliberately taught cognitive learning. Clearly, some rapprochement is needed, from the direction of the (more

cognitively sophisticated) psychology of learning to the (more contextually sophisticated) anthropology of learning (Erickson, 1982: 173).

In response to the concerns stated by Erickson and others, empowerment research has become a top priority for research organizations and individual scientists in the last five years. The use of cultural anthropology (and ethnographic research methods) and psychology in applied research projects whose purposes are to study people infected with AIDS, homeless families, dropouts, drug addicts, the impact of inequities in the health care system, the treatment of special education students, and the educational training of minority single-mothers, just to mention a few examples, show us the significance of interdisciplinary applied social science research.

Interdisciplinary Approaches to Action Research

Interdisciplinary research on minority dropouts can become a powerful tool in the implementation of educational reform, as long as the reform reflects genuine concern for the culture of minorities. Researchers can be instrumental in converting minority failure into success, provided they understand the roles of culture and social class in determining minority students' chances of success. Beyond the commitment to apply their analytical skills to real life issues, researchers must be compassionate in understanding the predicament of minority children, who are clearly not responsible for their academic underachievement or for their problems in adjusting to American social instructions. Researchers must also make a commitment to the principles of educational equity, whose very foundations require appreciation for minority languages and cultures. Finally, researchers will need a great deal of theoretical flexibility and persistence as they study the elusive role of cultural values in the acquisition of academic knowledge.

Sociologists, anthropologists and psychologists (Spindler and Spindler, 1987a, 1987b, 1989; Mehan, Hertwick and Meihls, 1986; Tharp and Gallimore, 1989; Cole and D'Andrade, 1982, and others) are indeed at the crossroads of epistemological and theoretical controversies, and they become involved in applied research with implications for educational reform. Some anthropologists have stated their concern for the quality of education for minorities and stated the need to capitalize on children's culture and language in order to improve the quality of instruction (Cummins, 1986, 1989; Trueba, 1989; Hatton, 1989; Spindler and Spindler, 1989). These approaches illustrate action research whose ultimate purpose is to enhance people's chances of participating in the American democratic system through empowerment processes based on learning. Isn't this precisely what thousands of immigrants seek as they face the dangers and tribulations in crossing American borders? Why should research sponsored by public institutions be deprived of this most fundamental philosophy and become insensitive to the main goal of all of our social institutions?

Sociologists offer good examples of ways in which we can link the macro-/micro-analytical, along with the basic/applied approaches. The work by Mehan, Hertwick and Meihls (1986) and by more recent educational sociologists, notably Bidwell and Friedkin (1988), can help researchers and educators in this task. Bidwell and Friedkin (1988) have shown how ethnohistorical analysis can help to establish links across methodological and theoretical preferences in sociology. Before 1900, sociologists such as Lester Ward and Albion Small viewed education as an instrument of social progress, rejecting the idea that curriculum should be structured according to presumed differential mental abilities (Bidwell and Friedkin, 1988). Durkheim's fundamental view of schooling was that schools were the normal instrument for socializing children into obedience to authority. In contrast, Sorokin (1927) began to look at upward social mobility and educational level, arguing that:

> when families command the economic and cultural resources required for social participation, the aggregate result is a very high level of status inheritance from one generation to the next and strong ascriptive biases in the distribution of life chances and social standing (Bidwell and Friedkin, 1988:452).

Sorokin did not seem to believe that education was a significant force in leveling or democratizing American society when he stated that: 'The school, even the most democratic school, open to everybody, if it performs its task properly, is a machinery of the "aristocratization" and stratification of society, not of "leveling" and "democratization"' (Sorokin, 1927:189-190). Both radical reformists from Neo-Marxist ranks and those from liberal mainstream ranks view the educational process as determining resource allocation on the basis of assumed potential of students, which in turn is the basis for tracking. It has also been agreed that overall student attainment correlates with tracking (Cicourel and Kitsuse, 1963).

According to Bidwell and Friedkin:

> To take the United States as a case in point, one would expect that
> after so many years of public and professional debate about
> equality of educational opportunity, American elementary and
> high schools would have taken effective steps against ascriptive
> biases in educational opportunities and achievement. Instead,
> American common schools seemingly transmit these biases,
> strengthening them in the process (Bidwell and Friedkin,
> 1988: 467).

Most importantly, failing to observe obvious patterns of educational
and social progress, as they are characterized by cultural or subcultural
differences within and across ethnic groups, is another way of neglecting to
identify the fundamental power of cultural values, as well as ignoring the
nature of cultural conflict during the process of educational and economic
development of minorities.

Social and Cognitive Development

While sociologists have made considerable progress in creating cooperative
approaches to study the differential achievement of minorities, they have
left out the role of culture. The more recent writings of psychologists,
educated in the anthropological tradition of ethnographic work in schools
and theoretically involved in Neo-Vygotskian thinking, suggest ways to
conceptualize the workings of culture in the acquisition of knowledge.
Tharp and Gallimore state:

> In summary, the cognitive and social development of the child (to
> the extent that the biological substrate is present) proceeds as an
> unfolding of potential through the reciprocal influences of child
> and social environment. Through guided intervention, higher
> mental functions that are part of the social and cultural heritage
> of the child will move from the social plane to the psychological
> plane, from the intermental to the intramental, from the socially
> regulated to the self-regulated. The child, through the regulating
> actions and speech of others, is brought to engage in independent
> action and speech. In the resulting interaction, the child
> performs, through assistance and cooperative activity, at

developmental levels quite beyond the individual level of achievement (Tharp and Gallimore, 1989: 29–30).

One of the most difficult stages of development to explain is the transition from adequate performance with assistance to adequate performance without assistance, through self-regulated behavior. Tharp and Gallimore's interpretation of Vygotsky summarizes this stage as follows:

> In the beginning of the transformation to the intramental plane, the child need not understand the activity as the adult understands it, need not be aware of its reasons or of its articulation with other activities. For skills and functions to develop into internalized, self-regulated capacity, all that is needed is performance, through assisting interaction. Through this process, this child acquires the 'plane of consciousness' of the natal society and is socialized, acculturated, made human (Tharp and Gallimore, 1989: 30).

This statement is consistent with contemporary views of sociolinguists discussing the relationship between performance and competence and their order of appearance. Competence assumes the internalization of concepts and some degree of self-regulation. Yet in the acquisition of competence, there are different degrees of acculturation and different requirements of cultural knowledge before competence is acquired. Before Tzeltal children (Mayan speakers of a Uto-Aztecan language in the highland Chiapas, Mexico) are allowed to travel in the jungle alone, they must recognize different paths, the position of the sun, various sounds of animals, the time of the day to assess the amount of daylight still available in their journey, and must learn the skillful use of the machete for purposes of self-defense. Furthermore, after traveling with an older sibling, they will be left behind on purpose, to see if they recognize marks and turns in the road. Eventually, they become independent travelers under distant supervision. Are intellectual competence and critical thinking skills acquired in similar fashion? Tharp and Gallimore seem to suggest it. The requirement for successfully moving to the next stage of development is that the adult, or more knowledgeable peer, plays his/her role effectively. That is, without a teacher who understands children's cognitive development, children will not be able to unfold their full academic potential.

The transition from assisted to independent performance must be anticipated by the parent, teacher or more knowledgeable peer. The assisted performance prior to transition requires:

- Effective communication between child and adult/peer
- Shared cultural values and assumptions
- Common goals for activities.

While the child has a limited understanding of the activity, the task, and its goals, adults (or more capable peers) guide and model for the child, and the child imitates. Gradually the child understands an activity's components in their appropriate cultural context, along with the meaning and consequences of the activity; and, through culturally and linguistically appropriate interaction, the child develops a suitable cognitive structure, which is continuously revised with new experiences and feedback (Wertsch, 1985 and Tharp and Gallimore, 1989).

Culture in Activity Settings

The concept of 'activity setting' is important for understanding the role of culture in the acquisition of knowledge. Tharp and Gallimore explain that an 'activity setting' encompasses both internal (intra-mental, cognitive, intra-psychological) features and external (motoric, inter-psychological, environmental) features: 'Maintaining a unit of analysis that incorporates simultaneously all these features — features that social science has always separated — requires some discipline of tought' (Tharp and Gallimore, 1989: 73).

To explain the activity setting, Tharp and Gallimore (1989: 74–79) have devised the five 'Ws' — who, what, when, where, and why — of the activity setting. Following the order and issues outlined by Tharp and Gallimore, with special reference to our discussion, will help the reader to identify the significance of culture during the acquisition of knowledge and the academic socialization of children.

Who. The persons involved in the activity setting are an integral part of the sociocultural environment in which children grow up; each culture, of course, has unique characteristics. The extended family unit for Hmong children, based on inclusion of the parents' families — originally male siblings who belong to the same patri-clan, but later extended to the wife's relatives — is different from the *maloca* (extended patrilineal clan of Tukanoan children living on the banks of the Amazon river). The *maloca* is formed by male siblings' nuclear families created through marriages by capture. In these *malocas* a child is exposed to as many as six different languages due to the nature of these clans. The sociocultural context for a low-income ghetto family headed by a single mother is completely different from that of an upper-class family in which the father is a neurosurgeon and the mother is a corporate lawyer. Therefore, the sociocultural unit, within which a child learns to participate in social activities, involves individuals who have culturally defined role relationships.

What. The 'what' of the activity includes an operation (description of the nature of the activity) and the way the operation is executed. Both the operation and the process of execution are defined within the culture of the family and community. A Tzeltal child from Chiapas, Mexico, who at 8 year old baby-sits for two siblings and is left alone in the jungle for six or seven hours while his parents cultivate their land, must engage in activities that will enhance his survival and those of his siblings. He must soon learn about snakes and which plants cure snake bites, how to fetch wood for the fire, to throw stones at wildcats approaching his hut, and to keep his siblings in sight, feeding them *atole* (corn gruel) and remaining stoically strong when hunger and pain abound. Similarly, but in a different cultural environment, a 'latch-key' child must learn how to survive in a downtown New York City apartment, and when and how to deal with strangers. The actual content of the operations, and the method for carrying out each operation, would clearly lead each of these children to different types of knowledge and skills, because the activity settings are very different, in spite of the fact that both aim at maximizing survival. Similarly, the role of adults and older siblings in the actual process of socialization would be critically different. Finally, if the latch-key child were placed in the jungle, and the Tzeltal child in the New York apartment, neither one would know what to do. Their knowledge and experience are intricately woven into their cultures and their activity settings.

Actual patterns of behavior learned in one setting are built on daily cultural experience and understanding. This understanding is in turn taken into the intra-mental plane to permit the child to structure cognitively that knowledge and experience so they may be applied in a future setting. The child's ability to link cognitively structured experiences to actual challenges faced in daily life, and to construct appropriate responses in the home situation, is built upon cultural patterns that are learned, internalized and independently generated. This is precisely why cultural congruence and values are essential for the acquisition of knowledge, and why, in situations of drastic cultural change, children are unable to acquire the type of new knowledge that is built upon a set of cultural experiences and values unknown to the child.

When. In the human life cycle there are critical events that mark important points: birth, puberty, mating, parenting, and death are some examples. These events are defined and emphasized ritualistically according to the norms of each culture. The experience in refugee camps and current secondary migration waves of Hmong families have not discouraged them from striving to maintain traditional ceremonies associated with the cultivation of crops and the major life events. Changes in religion from the cult of the ancestors to Protestant religion have also changed traditions. For a Mexican Catholic family, baptism brings together large numbers of relatives who congregate for the mass and baptism ceremonies at church and then participate in a feast. New relationships are born that day; there is a new *Padrino* and *Madrina* (Godfather and Godmother) for the child, who becomes the *Compadre* and *Comadre* (Co-father and Co-mother) of the parents. The baptized child's parents build social networks on the basis of these relationships, and the child will be taught to be a good godchild. The lessons associated with the baptism activity setting take place only during this critical event. There are cultural equivalents for other groups.

When a family is uprooted and forced to move from place to place, many of the culturally-grounded lessons, which would normally take place in the household with the extended family present, gradually become simplified or are omitted. Worse, when a family is attempting to adjust to different cultural settings and is not yet settled in any particular one, children are torn between the home learning environment and the outside social environment. There is a cultural gap, along with very unstable activity settings, both of which can decrease a child's motivation to learn. In some cases, there is no motivation to learn lessons in home culture activity settings, because these settings are perceived by people representing the dominant society as having little value. Today many Hmong feel the need to hide in order to perform their traditional wedding ceremonies, which take place at an early age. Hmong girls, whose marriages are arranged by their parents, are seen as victims by American society, and the lessons of appropriate behavior, which are culturally prescribed for Hmong women during the wedding ceremonies, are devalued in the face of American objections and questioning of the marriage validity.

Where. Ritual, symbolic, cultural activities and the acquisition of cultural knowledge are intimately related to places, times and people. Uprooting a family, moving them to an unfamiliar environment and attempting to socialize their children to patterns of behavior which oppose the cultural values of the dominant society are as difficult as the school's effort to socialize culturally different children into an American lifestyle. For children to integrate values, or to compartmentalize opposed values, the 'where' of what is learned is essential, permitting children to map out cognitively different interpretations of experience. Linguistic and cultural code-switching becomes a temporary survival strategy, indicating lack of linguistic skills in the second language. It requires time, effort and support on the part of schools and parents to switch the linguistic and cultural code.

Why. The 'why' deals with the fundamental question of motivation to learn and comprehend (Tharp and Gallimore, 1989: 164–191). In order to acquire and structure new knowledge and use it in the two planes (intra-psychological and inter-psychological), there must be a strong cultural value associated with the effort involved. This is the critical area of goal determination and orientation which fits into the general culturally-defined purpose of living, succeeding, and doing anything we do. The motivation for literacy may appear self-evident in a middle-class, industrial, technological society; it comes naturally. People read every day, they communicate through notes, use computers, continue their education, check on their children's reading skills, and so forth.

Gradually, children grow up with the idea that reading is a part of life and an essential instrument of progress. Learning reading and writing skills for a child who comes from an illiterate family raises a lot of questions regarding 'why'. The more a child reads material that has no relationship to a familiar cultural environment (the who, what, when, and where), the more difficult it will be for him or her to draw meaning from that material and become motivated to read more.

There are important implications of this theory of activity setting. First, it shows that there is no need to construct stereotypical theories about personality types fitting only certain kinds of ethnic groups. Second, it suggests that the stratification and sociocultural differences within ethnic groups render such efforts and theories unproductive, empirically unsubstantiated, and of questionable usefulness. What we need is to search for a solid theory of culture in order to explain the crucial role of cultural values in the learning process, and how culture is intimately linked to the development of children's cognitive skills. A Neo-Vygotskian perspective can be highly instrumental in explaining the role of culture in learning.

Reform in Teacher Education

The need for teacher education reform must start by recognizing the role of culture in teaching and learning, as well as in learning to teach — the extent to which culture operates as a filter for teachers' interpretation of students' perceptions, experiences, cognitive development, classroom participation and overall avhievement. Hatton (1989) discusses the use of Levi-Strauss' 'bricolage' metaphor as applied to teachers. She argues that:

> Teachers' work can be seen to parallel what intellectual and practical bricoleurs do. The parallel includes a tendency toward conservatism and limited creativity brought about by limited repertoires of means and limited approaches to repertoire enlargement on both intellectual and practical action. Importantly, characterizing teachers' work as bricolage, either on the plane of speculation or on the technical plane, involves accepting that it is typically a rational, even if limited, response to the circumstances in which teachers find themselves (Hatton, 1989: 84).

Teachers become technicians of a particular kind, scientists of the concrete, as a result of what Hatton calls 'anticipatory socialization', which takes place during many years of schooling and preservice experience as pupils. This experience fosters a more imitative process than a reflective or analytic one. New teachers gradually mimic without reflection on the roles of their own teachers. This type of socialization may lead to an inability of new teachers to confront fundamental issues regarding the instructional effectiveness, the implications of their own teaching strategies, and the incongruity of teaching minority students with techniques used by role models with mainstream students. Intuitive ways of teaching mainstream children may work, because there are common cultural assumptions and effective communication through a mutual language and culture.

This is not the case with minority children. The unexpected outcomes in teaching minority children with methods used for mainstream ones seem to come as a surprise to many teachers who did not work before with minorities (Hatton, 1989: 87–92). The tendency is to blame minority children for their failure to learn. Teachers may be aware of the cultural conflict and communicative problems minority children have, but they don't see those problems as being partially created by their teaching, or in any way having implications for reform. How can new teachers understand their part in the cultural conflict affecting the instruction process? How can they bypass this conflict and effectively transfer the knowledge and values students need to achieve? How can teachers identify those students who continue to function with a different set of cultural assumptions and experiences?

Neo-Vygotskian Theory of Assisted Performance

In an effort to develop a theoretically-grounded and more conscious approach to teacher education, whereby teachers learn socially-based theories about cognitive developments and design culturally-congruent instructional strategies, Tharp and Gallimore have pursued Neo-Vygotskian theory of assisted performance (1989). This approach seems to be most promising and deserves some explanation. Inspired by Lev Semyonovich Vygotsky (1962, 1978), Soviet psychologists and Neo-Vygotskians in the United States and Europe (see references in Wertsch, 1985; Tharp and Gallimore, 1989) have advanced theories intimately linking the development of higher mental operations to sociocultural activities through language.

Vygotsky viewed language as a symbolic system mediating thought and action, as well as an instrument for the development of thinking skills. Thus, the mastery of language was seen by Vygotsky as a measure of mental development. He emphasized the active role of the learner in determining his/her area of most possible (or probable) cognitive development (called the 'zone of proximal development' or ZPD). The learner exercises control of his ZPD through linguistic responses during learning activities. However, in order for the learner to respond, communication between teacher and learner must be culturally meaningful. The role that culture plays in communication during learning activities is essential to the process of transmission.

According to Wertsch (1987), Vygotsky's position clearly recognizes the instrumental role of culture in the use of specific means of communication during adult–child interaction. Language and culture are inseparable in the process of mediation between social and mental processes that constitute teaching and learning. Furthermore, language and culture continue to play a key role in the organization of cognitive tasks, the development of critical thinking skills, and the process of creative thinking.

One of the theoretical pillars of Vygotskian theory is that learning occurs in two planes, in the social or inter-psychological plane, and in the mental or intra-psychological plane. These two planes are mutually supportive and stand in a symbiotic relationship. Consequently, the sociocultural context of learning becomes critical in the acquisition and organization of new concepts and concept relationships. The reason is that within specific sociocultural contexts in which there is a network of relationships, constituting a supportive learning environment, a child learns to use symbolic systems (primarily language) shared with other members of the sociocultural group. This sociocultural group can be termed the micro-sociological unit of a child's interaction. It is precisely in the selection and interpretation of symbolic systems (called by Vygotsky 'mediational means') that children identify, classify and use culture-specific and culturally defined items. Ultimately, the embeddedness of language, culture and cognition rests on their multiple interrelationships, which surface during the process of communication.

If the choice and interpretation of symbols during communication bring together language, culture and cognition, it is also important to note with Wertsch that 'people privilege the use of one mediational means over others' and that 'we need to combine the analysis of collectively organized mediational means with the analysis of interpsychological functioning'. Consequently, if 'choice of mediational means is a major determinant of how thinking and speaking can proceed, then processes whereby groups make decisions (either implicitly or explicitly) about these means should become a focus of our research' (Wertsch, 1987: 20–21). Furthermore, according to Wertsch, *culture either determines or at least it facilitates a conscious, collective choice of communicative strategies.* Thus if we want to study memory, thinking, attention, or other facets of human consciousness, 'we must begin by recognizing the sociohistorical and cultural embeddedness of the subjects as well as investigators involved' (1987: 21–22). Coming from a psychologist who is one of the most eminent Vygotskian experts, this statement has a special significance.

It seems that is we choose a Neo-Vygotskian theoretical framework, we must recognize that symbolic systems are presumed to mediate between the mind and outside reality, and that the development of the higher mental operations is an essential requirement for high academic achievement. Reality, however, is perceived and determined by culturally defined patterns and knowledge transferred from one generation to another, as well as by universal psychological processes which go beyond any individual or cultural group. Regardless of sociocultural affiliation, linguistic and social skills develop within some microsociological unit in which children grow (family, community, school and the peer groups).

In consequence, we can argue that, given the social organization of America, effective English literacy instruction requires specific cultural values and skills as much as the historical and academic knowledge usually acquired by association with mainstream members of America (Spindler and Spindler, 1982, 1987b). The work by Gumperz and Hymes (1964), Gumperz (1982, 1986), and Cook–Gumperz (1986) points at the inter-relationships between communication, literacy and culture. These inter-relationships parallel the embeddedness of language, culture and cognition alluded to above. The roots of such interrelationships are in the collective sharing of socioculturally defined symbolic systems of communication. Literacy is rightfully called a 'socially constructed phenomenon' (Cook–Gumperz, 1986: 1). As a socially constructed phenomenon, literacy levels correspond to people's place in the social, economic and political institutes determining power hierarchies and access to resources. Conversely, social institutions, including the technological, industrial and military complexes, depend not only only on people's overall levels of literacy, but they also influence the quality and the direction of school curricula.

Achievement Motivation in Minorities

Directly or indirectly many recent anthropological studies have been based on the work by DeVos (1967, 1973, 1980, 1982, 1983; DeVos and Wagatsuma, 1966; Wagatsuma and DeVos, 1984). DeVos' insights into the psychosocial and cultural factors of differential motivation and achievement of minorities have inspired studies by Ogbu (1974, 1978, 1981, 1982, 1983, 1987a, 1987b), Suarez-Orozco (1987, 1989), Deyhle (1987), Gibson (1987) and others who use a 'cultural ecological perspective'. This perspective views social, economic and political forces (characteristic of previous literature — see Bowles and Gintis, 1976) as crucial in explaining the educational performance of oppressed groups.

DeVos' contribution to our understanding of the dynamics of achievement motivation is related to his use of broad comparative and analytical frameworks, in which he looks at cultural patterns of a given social group in order to explain culturally-based individual behavior in other groups. He shows the significance of culture in the organization of individual behavior and personality, with particular reference to achievement motivation. While Neo-Vygotskians see the sophistication in the use of linguistic forms as a manifestation of academic achievement, DeVos' work consistently brings us to the realization that in order to arrive at the appropriate interpretation of people's cultural (linguistic) symbols, one must first identify the broader culturally-patterned social structures in which specific behaviors are observed and recorded (by means of projective techniques or through traditional ethnographic methods). Symbols, according to Neo-Vygotskians, are presumed to mediate between the mind and outside reality (Tharp and Gallimore, 1989).

The outside reality of observed behavior, however, is determined for entire collectivities by cultural factors transmitted from one generation to the next (DeVos, 1973, 1983 and Spindler and Spindler, 1987a, 1987b and

1989). While there are some important theoretical differences in the perspectives represented by Neo-Vygotskians as compared with those of anthropologists, there are also many similarities. Therefore, for the most part, these approaches are compatible and complementary to each other.

An integration of sociohistorical (Neo-Vygotskian) and anthropological perspectives is potentially a powerful instrument for applied educational research. If we accept the principle that effective instruction requires effective transmission of academic knowledge and cultural values associated with this knowledge, then the role of culture and cultural values is also evident. More importantly, if we want to analyze the differential academic achievement and cognitive development of minority students, then we need both the sociohistorical (Neo-Vygotskian) and anthropological (cross-cultural) theories.

One of the most effective methodological tools, which makes possible the use of both Neo-Vygotskian and cross-cultural approaches, is ethnographic research. Ethnographic methods place us face-to-face with the interpretation of behavior in cross-cultural settings. As applied to learning settings, the validity of ethnographic research requires us to establish linkages between social and cultural macro-structures and the specific behaviors under study. In order to make valid inferences regarding achievement motivation, and/or participation in learning activities, the ethnographer must provide a suitable social and cultural context which makes behavior understandable (see Rueda and Mehan, 1986; Trueba, Moll, Diaz and Diaz, 1984, G. Spindler, 1987; Spindler and Spindler, 1987a, 1987b; Deyhle, 1987; Trueba, 1987a, 1987b, 1987c, 1988a, 1988b, 1988c, 1989).

Vygotsky expects the child to take an active role in determining his/her 'zone of proximal development' (ZPD) and level of activity. Activity is understood by Vygotsky as an intellectual and social engagement unit composed of action and operations. Anthropologists view the child's productive engagement in mental or social activities in ways that are congruent with his/her home language and culture. For anthropologists, human activity acquires meaning and predictability through home socialization patterns and in conformity to the cultural values transmitted from generation to generation in a given sociocultural group. For Vygotsky children determine their individual ZDP in which they work comfortably by moving continuously between the inter-psychological and the intra-psychological planes (Griffin, Newman and Cole, 1981:8). For cultural anthropologists (for example, DeVos, Spindler and their associates) children's role in learning is understandable within the broader historical and ecological parameters of the life of an entire sociocultural group and of the immediate family which defines the role of children.

According to the theoretical perspectives of the psychologists and anthropologists mentioned above, all children normally succeed in learning if given the opportunity to interact socially within their range of ability in culturally congruent settings. If some children succeed in learning and others fail, then it follows that failure in learning is as 'systemic' as success, and must be interpreted as the lack of access to appropriate (within range) and culturally congruent learning situations. Indeed, it is not an individual failure of the child, but a failure of the social system to provide the child with an opportunity to learn. This failure of the system is a social and cultural phenomenon which can be best understood in its social, historical, political and economic roots. In other words, a child's underachievement must be placed in the macro-sociological context of the opportunity structure, the status of minority groups and the allocation of resources. By the same token, one cannot explain a child's underachievement by looking at problems in a single social institution (family, school, church, or income). The problem may be pervasive across institutions. Consequently, in order to overcome 'systemic failures', instructional interventions in the various learning contexts must be planned (Cole and Griffin, 1983: 71; DeVos, 1980, 1983; Spindler and Spindler, 1987b, 1989; Trueba and Delgado–Gaitan, 1988; Trueba, 1989).

The lack of culturally appropriate mechanisms that ease the transition from a rural to an urban environment — such as those available to the rural Japanese moving to the cities who develop pseudo-kinship ties (DeVos, 1973: 207) — may create cultural discontinuities and cognitive ambiguities resulting in underachievement. Children undergoing cultural discontinuities have limited options available. One of these options is to reject their language, their culture and themselves; or to pretend to have another ethnic identity (Trueba, 1988). An important explanation for the maladjustment of some minority children, as was the case of several Indo-chinese studied, was that students could not handle cognitive tasks that were disproportionately difficult or meaningless without special assistance. Because of their pre-arrival traumas they needed help in order to find their 'zones of proximal development' (ZPD) in the new language and culture, and to translate foreign concepts into culturally meaningful tasks. Why were the risks so high and the potential penalties for failure so severe? The answer was in the nature of their pre-arrival traumas and their unfamiliarity with the norms and expectations of American culture. Religious beliefs, family organization, adults' and children's roles are all presumed valid across cultures by school personnel. In fact, differences in the home culture were compounded by pre-arrival experiences and the 'degrading incidents', related to the broad sociohistorical factors of the life of refugees, and by the and by the social structure placing minorities at the bottom of the social ladder (DeVos, 1973, 1980, 1983; Freire and Macedo, 1987; Trueba, 1989; Suarez-Orozco, 1989). The insights of cultural anthropologists in discussing cultural conflicts (for example, DeVos, 1973: 374–376 and Suarez-Orozco, 1989) lead to a further examination of the role of culture and psychosocial factors of academic achievement in minorities.

Intervention-Research for Minority Education

Intervention-research is intended to gather and analyze data systematically in order to document the process and/or outcomes of innovative and successful programs designed to resolve specific problems. In education, for example, experimentation with new programs could consist of new teaching strategies, new curricular arrangements, combined student populations, different schedules, different space and/or locality, changes in instructors or instructors' role, new methodology and/or classroom organization. To study these programs qualitative research is uniquely suited.

There are various qualitative approaches to research, including ethnographic ones (see, for example, Goetz and LeCompte, 1984; Erickson, 1986; Werner and Schoepfle, 1987; Spindler and Spindler, 1987a and Wolcott, 1988). Ethnographic research has been particularly successful in the last three decades. The necessary and sufficient criteria for valid ethnographic research are discussed in the literature (Spindler and Spindler, 1987a: 17–33; Wolcott, 1987: 37–57). Based on current qualitative studies in educational anthropology and psychology, it seems necessary to reexamine the contributions of qualitative research in the face of the minority education needs. First, to gain a better understanding of the needs of minorities, one must be able to link broader structural factors (sociohistorical, political and economic) affecting the lives of minority students. Second, qualitative research must have some implications for educational practice. We do not want to view the role of researchers as simply ivory tower theoreticians who disregard the knowledge and experience of practitioners and field-based ethnographers (Hargreaves, 1985: 21–47). The following considerations may simplify the relationship of theory to practice and the very nature of applied social science research in education:

1. Qualitative research is essentially a scientific process intended to make observed behavior understandable by linking it to broader contextual sociohistorical, economic, and behavioral factors.

2. The validity or explanatory power of qualitative research depends on the researcher's ability to understand the relationship between macro- and micro-analytical levels of data collected, and to establish crosscultural comparisons and contrasts.
3. The goals of educational researchers using qualitative methods are best served by using approaches which connect explicitly macro- and micro-structural levels of data collection and analysis from an interdisciplinary perspective which can assist policy makers and practitioners.

Is it possible to transcend the dichotomy of macro-analysis and micro-analysis in pursuit of more powerful explanations for behavioral and cognitive phenomena that have both immediate pragmatic consequences as well as long-term effects? It is not only possible, but necessary. The nature of ethnographic inquiry demands it, because it requires the establishment of relationships between larger sets of empirical data and specific interactional phenomena. It also requires an explicit relationship between the broader theoretical framework and the specific inferences made at the interactional level. The validity of ethnographic research rests on the strength of those links and relationships across analytical levels. That is, without linking macro- and micro-sociological levels, one cannot make sound inferences — usually grounded in demonstrable evidence gathered through field-based methods (Spindler, 1987a: 17–23).

The very nature of social science inquiry as a scientific study (Wolcott, 1987, 1988), primarily through the use of field-based methods such as participant observation, interactional analysis, interviews, and ethnohistorical analysis, must retain a clear linkage between contextual information (social, political, historical, economic and cultural) and individual behavioral phenomena recorded (interactional patterns, participant structures, and sociolinguistic usages of a single event).

Teachers' Role in the Academic Success of Minorities

The ultimate goal of minority education intervention research is to help turn academic failure into success. In order to do this, school personnel must depart from the assumption that children's potential is inexhaustible, and that the avenues for school achievement are many and flexible. The role of teachers must be redefined in order to permit them continuously to assist children in the actual learning process. Consequently, teachers need not see themselves as 'managers', 'inspectors', or 'guardians' of school rules. Teachers may work side-by-side with children to anticipate their cognitive skill level, their degree of value internalization, and their readiness to move on to more complex levels of learning.

At the heart of effective construction of academic success for minority children is the development of systems of assistance through the activity settings mentioned earlier. Tharp and Gallimore (1989) explain that the 'activity setting is a unit of analysis that transcends individuals and provides a meaningful way to integrate culture, local contexts and individual function'. The classroom, playground, cafeteria, auditorium, indeed the entire school, is comprised of activity settings. These settings can be optimally used to develop certain kinds of skills which would have an impact on all other activities. For example, the development of spoken language in the context of discourse skills for inquiry is most important. The nature of language environment is crucial to the development of other skills related to language use. Adult assistance gradually decreases as the child becomes more self-sufficient, and in some schools this assistance is the focus of the instructional program (for example, in the Carpinteria program, alluded to by Cummins, 1986, and the Kamehameha program, discussed by Tharp and Gallimore, 1989, who offer a continuum of instructional strategies).

Tharp and Gallimore explain, in some detail, the nature of the assistance and the means of providing it to students: questioning, modeling, and providing feedback. Teachers or more capable peers can play the role of assistant during instruction, and they can create the necessary conditions and participant structures required for a culturally congruent interaction: overlapping speech, joint performance, informal turntaking, role playing, and others (Tharp and Gallimore, 1989). Other examples of development of learning environments conducive to student success are offered in the work of Moll and Diaz (1987), Au and Jordan (1981), Boggs (1985), Trueba (1987a, 1987b, 1988a, 1988c, 1989), and Trueba and Delgado–Gaitan (1988).

Creating a more suitable environment for learning in a school characterized by cultural diversity of students is not an easy task. La Playa had twenty-five different language groups at the time of the study, and continues to be a source of cultural shock for new minority students coming from rural countries, some as refugees. Teachers did manifest their concern for improving the learning environment of children, and wanted to help, but often they did not understand either the children or themselves in the context of classroom interaction. They knew there were cultural distances and misunderstandings, but often they discovered too late that there were serious consequences of these misunderstandings. Some children had been placed in special education classes and were stigmatized, others had become discouraged, and others survived with serious psychological damage (Trueba, 1988c). It seems that what American educators need is a culturally-based theory of academic success and an approach for healing students and teachers during the cultural shock experienced in schools as they make contact and attempt to build a learning environment which shares cultural values. This can be accomplished by cultural therapy (Spindler, 1963, 1982; Spindler and Spindler, 1987a, 1987b).

Cultural Therapy and Academic Success

The interpretation of 'cultural therapy' as advanced by the Spindlers presupposes an understanding of culture as being 'the organization of activities that one engages in that result in one's acquiring possessions, recognition, powers, status and satisfaction' (Spindler and Spindler, 1987c: 2). This definition of culture assumes that if learning is going to take place, it must be goal-oriented, and that goal-orientation is culturally determined. As a process, cultural therapy can take multiple forms. For example, it can take the form of group sessions in which videotaped interactions are seen on the screen and various possible interpretations are discussed from the points of view of different cultures. The use of the 'reflective cross-cultural analysis' in a group setting can also be part of cultural therapy. Another form is a face-to-face encounter between a cross-cultural expert (an anthropologist, a psychologist, or a counselor) and a person working in culturally diverse settings. The purpose of such encounter is to understand the contrasting cultural assumptions associated with the various interactional patterns observed, and the possible cultural conflict or misunderstanding resulting from such patterns.

The ultimate purpose of cultural therapy is to bring cross-cultural and intra-cultural behavioral understanding which can empower people to act with competence. One of the most essential elements of cultural therapy is assisted-performance by teachers and mentors during group or personal encounters.

Cultural therapy assumes that there is a clear relationship between the choice of specific activity settings (and ways to conduct them) and the expected outcomes of these activities. If the parties involved come from two opposed cultural perspectives (that of the child vs. that of the teacher), it is very likely that there will be cultural conflict. The underlying assumption is that people select activities precisely because they have goals which fit their cultural value systems; that is, their goals enhance their culture. In this sense, activity settings become *instrumental* (Spindler and Spindler, 1987c) to the attainment of cultural goals, as well as to the expression of cultural values. 'School activity settings are internalized by teachers as settings that help them attain their goals of power, recognition, status, and so forth.'

One of the reasons that there is much cultural conflict within the school and such a conspicuous need for cultural therapy is the rapid socio-cultural change that affects young people. There are parts of the United States, such as California, which become the revolving door for waves of immigrants, refugees, and marginal individuals (from both ethnic minority and mainstream low-income groups). The pace of modern industrial societies and economic instability create a difficulty for schools. In a matter of a few years entire school districts have changed their balance of ethnic minorities served, yet teachers and administrators have not been prepared for this change. They feel upset, bewildered, and unable to establish close personal relationships with children, who do not seem to share teachers' values and who do not respond in expected ways. Thus teachers become less capable of assisting minority children in academic performance, or less prepared to allow minority children to determine their 'zones of proximal development' through the selection of culturally appropriate activity settings. Indeed, teachers feel a great deal of pressure not to abandon traditional curriculum structure, even in the face of failure with minority students (Trueba, 1988a, 1988b, 1988c).

Cultural therapy is predicated on the important distinction between the *enduring self* and the *situated self* (Spindler and Spindler, 1987c: 4). In their study of Remstal in Schoenhausen, Germany, the Spindlers observed that the rapid change in people and cultural environment was coexistent with enduring characteristics of the classroom learning environment, and with the type of relationships between teachers and students. It was not until after several years of close observations that the contrast between the *enduring self*, which was 'equated with ideal-romantic instrumental choices and rationalizations' or with images of the traditional land and village life, and the *situated self*, 'equated with the pragmatic modality' of urban lifestyle in an industrial society, became clearly conceptualized as an integrating mechanism in the face of change. Thus, the Spindlers noted that 'instrumental competencies' were developed in response to life changes in the teachers and students, but at the same time a profound attachment to the *enduring self* of the early socialization period remained constant, providing psychological cohesiveness to individuals. This most significant insight allows us to engage in cultural therapy in the context of the school activity settings, in ways that permit children and school personnel to accommodate, compromise and adjust without having to deny their cultural heritage. The main goal of cultural therapy is to develop instrumental competence for functioning in new and diverse cultural environments without losing one's personal identity.

Children develop a sense of self-esteem and competence as a result of their experience of success. This experience is the result of actually mastering certain tasks executed in specific activity settings. Successful mastery is first gained through *assisted performance*, with the help of the teacher and peers, then gradually practiced independently through self-regulated psychological processes. To change a failing academic environment into a succeeding one, one must think about the observations made by the Spindlers:

> Minority children with various sociocultural backgrounds attend schools predicated on mainstream, largely middle class, and largely white Anglo Saxon North European Protestant cultural assumptions. Such children acquire deficits in self-esteem when they fail to master essential instrumentalities in this context. Their self-esteem is damaged not only by actual failure, but also by negative perceptions and low expectations of them by teachers and other students (Spindler and Spindler, 1987c: 5).

At the basis of mastering a task and the experience of success there is self-esteem, and one of the components of self-esteem is *self-efficacy*:

> We define self-efficacy as a prediction that one will be able to meet the demands of the situation effectively . . . Self-efficacy in our terms is an expectation that one can exhibit instrumental competence in the appropriate contexts (Spindler and Spindler, 1987c: 6)

It is conceivable that minority children and their teachers can develop new instrumental competencies by engaging in negotiated activity settings that permit them to succeed. Student success and teacher success are no more separable than the communicative effectiveness of either teacher or student. If children succeed, teachers feel they succeed too. Therefore, it is extremely important for teachers to realize that *they* are experiencing cultural shock when they try to function effectively with children who do not share their values and expectations. Academic success requires, then, that both teachers and children build learning environments in which success is possible for both. One way to build such a successful environment is through cultural therapy, which may be viewed as the process of 'conscientization' (Freire, 1973). That is, teachers and children must become consciously aware of their cultural identities, background, history and differences, in such a way that high levels of self-esteem are maintained. This awareness must permit teachers to facilitate children's understanding and integration of American cultural values, as well as to gain an understanding of the process of acculturation through which children are going.

Conclusion

Social scientists have discussed failure long enough. It is time to create theoretical models directed to success. One of the most eloquent statements, which arose in the context of discussing the nature of academic failure, was made by McDermott:

> Not all roads come to good endings . . . Now I am trying to move beyond the problem of school failure that has grown into a small industry involving millions of people measuring, documenting, remediating, and explaining the habits, values, and skills of the minority groups that contribute so heavily to their ranks of school failures (McDermott, 1987b: 361–2).

It is rather paradoxical that even the most liberal modern anthropologists, such as cultural ecologists who have been striving to move our thinking away from 'deficit' approaches, end up producing theoretical constructs that are seen by many as being stereotypic and driven by cultural or motivational deficit ideologies. Are not these ideologies contaminated by the 'blame the victim' syndrome? Perhaps what is wrong with current social science research (including anthropology) is its preoccupation with the politics of education, rather than with the practice of education.

While some speculate about success or failure, others create and document success through a theoretical frame outlined above. There is a profound lesson for educational anthropologists in McDermott's remarks and recent ethnographic work (see Spindler and Spindler, 1987a, 1987b; Goldman and McDermott, 1987; Moll and Diaz, 1987; Trueba, 1989; Trueba and Delgado–Gaitan, 1988; Tharp and Gallimore, 1989). The sheer fact of rapid reorganization of school failure into genuine academic success should have and does have consequences for the reorganization of our own theories and explanatory models. Aware of the limitation of ethnographic research, we must go back to it, refine methodological strategies and clarify conceptual priorities.

Most of all, we cannot overextend our evidence, or, even for the sake of claiming 'scientific' or explanatory status over other approaches, neglect the empirical support behind theoretical statements. Perhaps we will have to scale down our expectations regarding the value of one approach versus others. In the end, the strength of ethnographic research and its contribution to theory building (Spindler and Spindler, 1987a) will depend on the strength of each of the micro-analytical links of the inferential chains that form our macro-theoretical statements.

We must strive to understand the way culture works in the acquisition of new knowledge and the construction of successful learning environments. To this end the development of activity settings must take into consideration the need that teachers and students have for healing and coping with cultural shock. Cultural therapy is a concept that may be helpful in obtaining an integration of cultural values which we acquired in early socialization and the new values we acquire as we adjust to new environments. The experience of academic success, the mastering of instrumental competencies and the maintenance of high self-esteem are all related to this integration of deep-seated cultural values and the new ones we acquire in the process of adjustment.

Bibliography

AU, K. and JORDAN, C. (1981) 'Teaching reading to Hawaiian children: Finding a culturally appropriate solution', in TRUEBA, H., GUTHRIE, G. and AU, K. (eds), *Culture and the Bilingual Classroom: Studies in Classroom Ethnography*, Rowley, MA: Newbury House Publishers, Inc., pp. 139–52.

BERNATZIK, H. (1970) *Akha and Miao: Problems of Applied Ethnography in Farther India*, New Haven, CT: Human Relations Area Files.

BIDWELL, C. and FRIEDKIN, N. (1988) 'The sociology of education', in SMELSER, N. (ed.) *The Handbook of Sociology*, Newbury Park, CA: Sage Publications, pp. 449–71.

BLIATOUT, B. T., DOWNING, B. T., LEWIS, J. and YANG, D. (1988) *Handbook for Teaching Hmong-speaking Students*, Folsom, CA: Folsom-Cordova Unified School District.

BOGGS, S. T. (1985) *Speaking, Relating, and Learning: A Study of Hawaiian Children at Home and at School*, Norwood, NJ: Ablex Publishing Corp.

BORISH, S. (1988) 'The winter of their discontent: Cultural compression and decompression in the life cycle of the Kibbutz adolescent', in TRUEBA, H., DELGADO-GAITAN, C. (eds) *School and Society: Teaching Content Through Culture*, New York: Praeger, pp. 181–99.

BOWLES, S. and GINTIS, H. (1976) *Schooling in Capitalist America: Educational Reform and the Contradictions of Economic Life*, NY: Basic Books.

CICOUREL, A. and KITSUSE, J. (1963) *The Educational Decision-makers*, Indianapolis, IN: Bobbs-Merrill.

COLE, M. and D'ANDRADE, R. (1982) 'The influence of schooling on concept formation: Some preliminary conclusions', *The Quarterly Newsletter of the Laboratory of Comparative Human Cognition*, **4**(2), pp. 19–26.

COLE, M. and GRIFFIN, P. (1983) 'A socio-historical approach to re-mediation', *The Quarterly Newsletter of the Laboratory of Comparative Human Cognition*, **5**(4), pp. 69–74.

COLE, M. and SCRIBNER, S. (1974) *Culture and Thought: A Psychological Introduction*, NY: Basic Books.

COOK-GUMPERZ, J. (ed.) (1986) *The Social Construction of Literacy*, Cambridge, England: Cambridge University Press.

COOPER, R. (1979) 'The Yao Jua relationship: Patterns of affinal alliance and residence among the Hmong of Northern Thailand', *Ethnology*, **18**(2), pp. 173–81.

COOPER, R. (1986) 'The Hmong of Laos: Economic factors in the refugee exodus and return', in HENDRICKS, G. L., DOWNING, B. T. and DEINARD, A. S. (eds) *The Hmong in Transition*, New York, NY: Center for Migration Studies of New York, Inc. The Southeast Asian Refugee Studies of the University of Minnesota, pp. 23–40.

CUEVAS, G. (1984) 'Mathematics learning in English as a Second Language'. *Journal for Research in Mathematics Education*, **15**, 2, pp. 134–44.

CUMMINS, J. (1986) 'Empowering minority students: A framework for intervention', *Harvard Educational Review*, **56(1)**, pp. 18–35.

CUMMINS, J. (1989) 'Empowering minority students', California Association for Bilingual Education Publications.

CUSTODIO VEGA, A., OSA (1963) *Obras de San Augustin. Texto Bilinque. Tomo II. Las Confesiones.* Cuarta Edicion. Biblioteca de Autores Cristianos. Madrid, Spain: La Editorial Catolica.

D'ANDRADE, R. (1984) 'Cultural meaning systems', in SHWEDER, R. A. and LEINE, R. A. (eds), *Culture Theory*, Cambridge, England: Cambridge University Press, pp. 88–119.

DELGADO–GAITAN, C. (1987a) 'Traditions and transitions in the learning process of Mexican children: An ethnographic view', in SPINDLER, G. and L. (eds) *Interpretive ethnography of education: At home and abroad*, Hillsdale, NJ: Laurence Erlbaum Associates, Publishers, pp. 333–59.

DELGADO–GAITAN, C. (1987b) 'Parent perceptions of school: Supportive Environments for Children', in TRUEBA, H. (ed.) *Success or Failure?: Learning and the Language Minority Student*, Cambridge, MA: Newbury/Harper and Row, pp. 131–55.

DELGADO–GAITAN, C. (1989) *Literacy for Empowerment*, Basingstoke, England: The Falmer Press.

DEVOS, G. (1966) 'Essential elements of caste: Psychological determinants in structural theory', in DEVOS, A. and WAGATSUMA, H. (eds) *Japan's Invisible Race: Caste in Culture and Personality*, Berkeley, CA: University of California Press, pp. 332–84.

DEVOS, G. (1973) 'Japan's outcastes: The problem of the Burakumin', in WHITAKER, B. (ed.) *The Fourth World: Victims of Group Oppression*, NY: Schocken Books, pp. 307–27.

DEVOS, G. (1980) 'Ethnic adaptation and minority status', *Journal of Cross-Cultural Psychology*, **11**, pp. 101–24.

DEVOS, G. (1982) 'Adaptive strategies in U.S. Minorities', in JONES, E. and KORCHIN, S. J. (eds) *Minority Mental Health*, NY: Praeger, pp. 74–117.

DEVOS, G. (1983) 'Ethnic identity and minority status: Some psycho-cultural considerations', in JACOBSON–WIDDING, A. (ed.) *Identity: Personal and Socio-cultural*, Uppsala, Sweden: Almquist Wiksell Tryckeri AB, pp. 90–113.

DEVOS, G. (1984) 'Ethnic persistence and role degradation: An illustration from Japan', Paper read April 1984, at the American-Soviet Symposium on Contemporary Ethnic Processes in the USA and the USSR, New Orleans, LA.

DeVos, G. and Wagatsuma, H. (1966) *Japan's Invisible Race: Caste in Culture and Personality*, Berkeley, CA: University of California Press.

Deyhle, D. (1987) 'Learning Failure: Tests as gatekeepers and the culturally different child', in Trueba, H. (ed.) *Success or Failure?: Learning and the Language Minority Student*, New York, Newbury Publishers, a division of Harper and Row, pp. 85–108.

Diaz, S., Moll, L. and Mehan, H. (1986) 'Sociocultural resources in instruction: A context-specific approach', in *Beyond Language: Social and Cultural Factors in Schooling Language Minority Students*, Sacramento, CA: Bilingual Education Office, California State Department of Education, pp. 187–230.

Dunn, L. M. (1987) *Bilingual Hispanic Children on the U.S. Mainland: A Review of Research on Their Cognitive, Linguistic, and Scholastic Development*, Circle Pines, MN: American Guidance Service.

Durkheim, E. (1961) *Moral Education*, Glencoe, IL: Free Press.

Eisenstadt, S. N. (1954) *The Absorptions of Immigrants*, London, England: Routledge and Kegan Paul.

Erickson, F. (1982) 'Taught cognitive learning in its immediate environments: A neglected topic in the anthropology of education', *Anthropology and Education Quarterly*, **13(2)**, pp. 149–80.

Erickson, F. (1984) 'School literacy, reasoning, and civility: An anthropologist's perspective', *Review of Educational Research*, **54(4)**, pp. 525–44.

Erickson, F. (1986) 'Qualitative methods in Research on Teaching', in Wittrock, M. C. (ed.) *Handbook of Research on Teaching*, New York: Macmillan Publishing Co, pp. 119–58.

Erickson, F. (1987) 'Transformation and school success: The politics and culture of educational achievement', *Anthropology and Education Quarterly*, **18(4)**, pp. 335–56.

Florio-Ruane, S. (1988) 'The relation of family, community, and schooling in tomorrow's schools', Unpublished manuscript. Michigan State University, East Lansing, MI: Holmes Group.

Frake, C. (1964) 'Notes on queries in ethnography', *American Anthropologist*, **66(3)**, pp. 132–45.

Freire, P. (1973) *Pedagogy of the Oppressed*, NY: Seabury.

Freire, P. and Macedo, F. (1987) *Literacy: Reading the Word and the World*. A volume in the *Critical Studies in Education Series*, Freire, P. and Giroux, H. (eds) South Hadley, MA: Bergin and Garvey Publishers.

Fujita, M. and Sano, T. (1988) 'Children in American and Japanese day-care centers: Ethnography and reflective cross-cultural interviewing', in Trueba, H. and Delgado-Gaitan, C. (eds) *School and Society: Teaching Content Through Culture*, NY: Praeger, pp. 73–97.

Garrett, W. E. (1974) 'The Hmong of Laos: No place to run', *National Geographic*, **145(1)**, pp. 78–111.

Geddes, W. R. (1976) *Migrants of the Mountains*, Oxford, England: Clarendon Press.

GIBSON, M. (1987) 'The school performance of immigrant minorities: A comparative view', *Anthropology and Education Quarterly*, **18(4)**, pp. 262–75.

GIM, W. and LITWIN, T. (1980) *Indochinese Refugees in America: Profiles of Five Communities*, Washington, DC: United States Department of State, Executive Seminar in National and International Affairs.

GIROUX, H. (1983) 'Theories of reproduction and resistance in the new sociology of education: A critical analysis', *Harvard Educational Review*, **53(3)**, pp. 257–93.

GIROUX, H. and MCLAREN, P. (1986) 'Teacher education and the politics of engagement: The case of democratic schooling', *Harvard Educational Review*, **56(3)**, pp. 213–38.

GOETZ, J. P. and LE COMPTE, M. (1984) *Ethnography and Qualitative Design in Educational Research*, New York, NY: Academic Press.

GOLDMAN, S. and MCDERMOTT, R. (1987) 'The culture of competition in American schools', *Education and Cultural Process: Anthropological Approaches*, Second Edition, Prospect Heights, IL: Waveland Press, Inc., pp. 282–89.

GOLDMAN, S. and TRUEBA, H. (eds) (1987) *Becoming Literate in English as a Second Language: Advances in Research and Theory*. Norwood, NJ: Ablex Corp.

GOODENOUGH, W. (1971) *Culture, Language and Society*, An Addison-Wesley Module in Anthropology, 7, Reading, MA: Addison-Wesley Publishing Company, Inc.

GRAHAM, D. C. (1937) 'The customs of the Ch'uan Miao', *Journal of the West China Border Research Society*, 9, pp. 18–20.

GRIFFIN, P., NEWMAN, D. and COLE, M. (1981) 'Activities, actions and formal operations: A Vygotskian analysis of a Piagetian task', Unpublished manuscript. Laboratory of Comparative Human Cognition, University of California, San Diego, CA.

GUMPERZ, J. (ed.) (1982) *Language and Social Identity*, Cambridge, MA: Cambridge University Press.

GUMPERZ, J. (1986) 'Interactional sociolinguistics in the study of schooling', in COOK–GUMPERZ, J. (ed.) *The Social Construction of Literacy*, Cambridge, MA: Cambridge University Press, pp. 45–68.

GUMPERZ, J. and HYMES, D. (eds) (1964) 'The ethnography of communication', *American Anthopologists*, **66(6)**.

GUMPERZ, J. and HYMES, D. (1972) *Directions in Socio-linguistics: The Ethnography of Communication*, New York, NY: Holt, Rinehart, and Winston.

HAINES, D. (1982) 'Mismatch in the resettlement process: The Vietnamese family versus the American housing market', *Journal of Refugee Resettlement*, **1(1)**, pp. 15–19.

HALPERN, J. and KUNSTADTER, P. (1967) 'Laos: Introduction', in KUNSTADTER, P. (ed.) *Southeast Asian Tribes, Minorities and Nations*, Princeton, NJ: Princeton University Press.

HARGREAVES, A. (1985) 'The Micro-Macro problem in the sociology of education', in BURGESS, R. G. (ed.) *Issues in Educational Research: Qualitative Methods*, Basingstoke, England: The Falmer Press, pp. 21–47.

HATTON, E. (1989) 'Levi-Strauss's *Bricolage* and theorizing teachers' work', *Anthropology and Education Quarterly*, **20(2)**, 74–96.

HEIMBACH, E. (1979) *White Hmong-English Dictionary*, Ithaca, NY: Southeast Asia Program, Cornell University.

HORNBERGER, N. (1988) 'Iman Chay?: Quechua Children in Peru's Schools', in TRUEBA, H. and DELGADO–GAITAN, C. (eds) *School and Society: Teaching Content Through Culture*, NY: Praeger, pp. 99–117.

JACOBS, L. (1986) 'Fieldnotes in La Playa', Unpublished manuscript. University of California, Santa Barbara, CA.

JACOBS, L. (1987) *Differential Participation and Skill Level in Four Hmong Third Grade Students: The Social and Cultural Context of Teaching and Learning*. Doctoral Dissertation. Graduate School of Education. University of California, Santa Barbara, CA.

JENSEN, A. R. (1981) *Straight Talk about Mental Tests*. New York, NY: The Free Press.

JOHNSON, C. (1985) *Dab Neeg Hmoob (Myths, Legends and Folk Tales from the Hmong of Laos)*, St. Paul, MN: Linguistics Department, Macalester College.

JUSTUS, J. (1976) 'Processing Indochinese refugees', in BRYCE–LAPORT, R. and COUCH, S. (eds) *Exploratory Fieldwork on Latino Migrants and Indochinese Refugees*, Washington, DC: Smithsonian Institute, pp. 76–100.

KELLER, S. (1975) *Uprooting and Social Change: The Role of Refugees in Development*, Delhi, India: Manohar Book Service.

KELLY, G. (1977) *From Vietnam to America: A Chronicle of the Vietnamese Immigration to the United States*, Boulder, CO: Westview Press.

KIRTON, E. S. (1985) *The Locked Medicine Cabinet: Hmong Health Care in America*, Doctoral dissertation, Department of Anthropology, University of California, Santa Barbara, CA.

KIRTON, E. S. (1987) 'Fieldnotes taken in La Playa Community', Unpublished manuscript, University of California, Santa Barbara, CA.

KUNZ, E. (1973) 'The refugee in flight: Kinetic models and forms of displacement', *International Migration Review*, **17(1)**, pp. 4–33.

LARTEGUY, J. (1979) *La Fabuleuse Aventure du Peuple de l'Opium*, Paris, France: Presses de la Cite.

LECOMPTE, M. and GOETZ, J. (1984) 'Ethnographic data collection in evaluation research', in FETTERMAN, D. (ed.) *Ethnography in Educational Evaluation*, Beverly Hills, CA: Sage Publications, pp. 37–59.

LEE, G. Y. (1982) 'Minority policies and the Hmong', in STUART-FOX, M. (ed.) *Contemporary Laos: Studies in the Politics and Society of the Lao People's Democratic Republic*, New York, NY: St. Martin's Press, pp. 199–219.

LEE, G. Y. (1986) 'Culture and adaptation: Hmong refugees in Australia' in HENDRICKS, G., DOWNING, B. and DEINARD, A. (eds) *The Hmong in Transition*, New York, NY: The Center for Migration Studies, pp. 55–72.

LEMOINE, J. (1972) *Un Village Hmong Vert du Haut Laos*. Paris, France: Centre Nationale de la Recherche Scientifique.

LI, J. (1988) 'Txuj ci Hmoob ntsa iab nto moo mus thoob qab ntuj' ('Our rich and colorful culture'), *Haiv Hmoob (Hmong Magazine)*, **4**(2), pp. 1–2.

LIS, N. (1986b) *Vim Leejtwg*, Australia: Roojntawv Neejmhoob.

LIS, N. (1987) *Txoj Sawlhub*, Australia: Roojntawv Neejmhoob.

LIS, N. (Lee, Pao) (1986a) *Lub neej daitaw*, Australia: Roojntawv Neejmhoob.

LIU, W., LAMANNA, M. and MURATA, A. (1979) *Transition to Nowhere*, Nashville, TN: Charter House.

MACIAS, J. (1987) 'The hidden curriculum of Papago Teachers: American Indian strategies for mitigating cultural discontinuity in early schooling', in SPINDLER, G. and L. (eds) *Interpretive Ethnography of Education: At Home and Abroad*, Hillsdale, NJ: Lawrence Erlbaum Associates, pp. 363–80.

McCOY, A. (1970) 'French colonialism in Laos, 1893–1945', in ADAMS, N. and McCOY, A. (eds) *Laos: War and Revolution*, New York, NY: Harper and Row, pp. 67–99.

McDERMOTT, R. (1987a) 'Achieving school failure: An anthropological approach to illiteracy and social stratification', in SPINDLER, G. (ed.) *Education and Cultural Process: Anthropological Approaches*, Second Edition. Prospect Heights, IL: Waveland Press, Inc., pp. 173–209.

McDERMOTT, R. (1987b) 'The explanation of minority school failure, again'. *Anthropology and Education Quarterly*, **18**(4), pp. 361–364.

McINNES, K. (1981) 'Secondary migration among the Indochinese', *Journal of Refugee Resettlement*, **1**(3), pp. 36–42.

MEHAN, H., HERTWICK, A. and MEIHLS, J. L. (1986) *Handicapping the Handicapped: Decision Making in Students' Educational Careers*, Stanford, CA: Stanford University Press.

MOHATT, G. and ERICKSON, F. (1981) 'Cultural differences in teaching styles in an Odawa school: A sociolinguistic approach', in TRUEBA, H., GUTHRIE, G. and AU, K. (eds) *Culture and the Bilingual Classroom: Studies in Classroom Ethnography*, Rowley, MA: Newbury House, pp. 105–119.

MOLL, L. (1986) 'Writing as communicaiton: Creating strategic learning environments for students', *Theory to Practice*, **26**(2), pp. 102–8.

MOLL, L. and DIAZ, E. (1987) 'Change as the goal of educational research', *Anthropology and Education Quarterly*, **18**(4), pp. 300–11.

MONTERO, D. (1979) *Vietnamese Americans: Patterns of Resettlement and Socioeconomic Adaptation in the United States*, Boulder, CO: Westview Press.

MUECKE, M. (1982) 'In search of healers — Southeast Asian refugees in American health care system', *Western Journal of Medicine*, **139**(6), pp. 835–840.

MURPHY, H. B. M. (1955) *Flight and Resettlement*, Paris, France: UNESCO.

OFFICE OF REFUGEE RESETTLEMENT (1989) *Report to the Congress: Refugee Resettlement Program*, Washington, DC: US Government Printing Office.

OGBU, J. (1974) *The Next Generation: An Ethnography of Education in an Urban Neighborhood*, New York, NY: Academic Press.

OGBU, J. (1978) *Minority Education and Caste: The American System in Cross-cultural Perspective*, New York, NY: Academic Press.

OGBU, J. (1981) 'Origins of human competence: A cultural-ecological perspective', *Child Development*, 52, pp. 413–429.

OGBU, J. (1982) 'Cultural discontinuities and schooling', *Anthropology and Education Quarterly*, 13(4), pp. 290–307.

OGBU, J. (1983) 'Minority status and schooling in plural societies', *Comparative Education Review*, 27(2), pp. 168–190.

OGBU, J. (1987a) 'Variability in minority responses to schooling: Nonimmigrants vs. immigrants', in SPINDLER, G. and L. (eds), *Interpretive Ethnography of Education: At Home and Abroad*, Hillsdale, NJ: Lawrence Erlbaum Associates, pp. 255–78.

OGBU, J. (1987b) 'Variability in minority school performance: A problem in search of an explanation', *Anthropology and Education Quarterly*, 18(4), pp. 312–334.

OGBU, J. and MATUTE-BIANCHI, M. E. (1986) 'Understanding sociocultural factors: Knowledge, identity and school adjustment', in *Beyond Language: Social and Cultural Factors in Schooling Language Minority Students*, Sacramento, CA: Bilingual Education Office, California State Department of Education, pp. 73–142.

PLANT, J. (1979) 'The impact of the CETA program on Indochinese refugees: A comparative analysis', in STOPP, G. H. and HGUYEN NANH HUNG, (eds) *Proceedings of the First Annual Conference on Indochinese Refugees*, Fairfax, VA: George Mason University.

RICHARDS, J. B. (1987) 'Learning Spanish and classroom dynamics: School failure in a Guatamalan Maya community', in TRUEBA, H. T. (ed.) *Success or Failure?: Learning and the Language Minority Student*, NY: Newbury Publishers, a Division of Harper and Row, pp. 109–30.

RUEDA, R. and MEHAN, H. (1986) 'Metacognition and passing: Strategic interaction in the lives of students with learning disabilities', *Anthropology and Education Quarterly*, 17(3), pp. 139–165.

RUEDER, STEPHEN, *et al.* (1987) *Hmong Resettlement Study, Volume I*, Washington, DC: US Department of Health and Human Services.

SAVINA, F. M. (1930) *Histoire de Miao*, Hong Kong: Societe des Missions Etrangeres de Paris.

SCHEIN, L. (1986) 'The Miao in contemporary China: A preliminary overview', in HENDRICKS, G. L., DOWNING, B. T. and DEINARD, A. J. (eds), *The Hmong in Transition*, New York, NY: Center for Migration Studies of the University of Minnesota, pp. 73–85.

SCOTT, G. (1979) 'The Hmong refugees of San Diego: Initial strategies of adjustment', in STOPP, G. H. and HUNG, H. N. (eds), Proceedings of the first annual conference on Indochinese refugees. Fairfax, VA: George Mason University.

SCRIBNER, S. and COLE, M. (1981) *The Psychology of Literacy*, Cambridge, MA: Harvard University Press.

SHARP, R. and GREEN, A. (1975) *Education and Social Control*, London, England: Routledge and Kegan Paul.

SHULMAN, L. (1987a) 'Knowledge and teaching: Foundations of the new reform', *Harvard Educational Review*, 57(1), pp. 1–22.

SHULMAN, L. (1987b) 'Sounding an alarm: A reply to Sockett', *Harvard Educational Review*, 57(4), pp. 473–82.

SMALLEY, W. A. (1986) 'Stages of Hmong cultural adaptation', in HENDRICKS, G. L., DOWNING, B. T. and DEINARD, S. (eds) *The Hmong in Transition*, New York, NY: Center for Migration Studies of the University of Minnesota, pp. 7–22.

SOCKETT, H. (1987) 'Has Shulman got the strategy right?' *Harvard Educational Review*, 57(2), pp. 208–19.

SOROKIN, P. A. (1927) *Social and Cultural Mobility*, New York, NY: Harper and Row.

SPINDLER, G. (1963) *Education and Culture: Anthropological Approaches*, New York, NY: Holt, Rinehart and Winston.

SPINDLER, G. (1974) 'Schooling in Schoenhausen: A study of cultural transmission and instrumental adaptation in an urbanizing German village', in SPINDLER, G. (ed.) *Education and Cultural Process: Toward an Anthropology of Education*, New York, NY: Holt, Rinehart and Winston, Inc., pp. 230–71.

SPINDLER, G. (1977) 'Change and continuity in American core cultural values: An anthropological perspective', in DERENZO, G. D. (ed.) *We the People: American Character and Social Change*, Westport, CT: Greenwood, pp. 20–40.

SPINDLER, G. (1982) *Doing the Ethnography of Schooling: Educational Anthropology in Action*, New York, NY: Holt, Rinehart and Winston.

SPINDLER, G. (1987) 'Why have minority groups in North America been disadvantaged by their schools?' in SPINDLER, G. (ed.) *Education and Cultural Process: Anthropological Approaches,* Second Edition, Prospect Heights, IL: Waveland Press, Inc.

SPINDLER, G. and SPINDLER, L. (1982) 'Roger Harker and Schöenhausen: From familiar to strange and back again', in SPINDLER, G. (ed.) *Doing the Ethnography of Schooling: Educational Anthropology in Action*, New York, NY: Holt, Rinehart and Winston, pp. 21–46.

SPINDLER, G. and SPINDLER, L. (1983) 'Anthropologists' view of American culture', *Annual Review of Anthropology*, 12, pp. 49–78.

SPINDLER, G. and SPINDLER, L. (1987a) *The Interpretive Ethnography of Education: At Home and Abroad*, Hillsdale, NJ: Lawrence Erlbaum Associates.

SPINDLER, G. and SPINDLER L. (1987b) 'Cultural dialogue and schooling in Schoenhausen and Roseville: A comparative analysis', *Anthropology and Education Quarterly*, **18(1)**, pp. 3–16.

SPINDLER, G. and SPINDLER, L. (1987c) 'Why have minority groups in North America been disadvantaged by their schools?' in SPINDLER, G. (ed.) *Education and Cultural Process: Anthropological Approaches*, Second Edition. New York, NY: Holt, Rinehart and Winston, pp. 160–172.

STUART–FOX, M. (1986) *Laos: Politics, Economics and Society*, London, England: Frances Pinter.

SUAREZ–OROZCO, M. (1987) 'Towards a psychosocial understanding of Hispanic adaptation to American schooling', in TRUEBA, H. (ed.) *Success or Failure: Linguistic Minority Children at Home and in School*, New York, NY: Harper and Row, pp. 156–68.

SUAREZ–OROZCO, M. M. (1989) *Central American Refugees and U.S. High Schools: A Psychosocial Study of Motivation and Achievement*, Stanford, CA: Stanford University Press.

THAO, C. (1982) 'Hmong migration and leadership in Laos and in the United States', in DOWNING, B. and OLNEY, D. (eds), *The Hmong in the West*, Minneapolis, MN: University of Minnesota, Southeast Asian Refugee Studies Project.

THARP, R. and GALLIMORE, R. (1989) *Rousing Minds to Life: Teaching, Learning and Schooling in Social Context*, Cambridge, England: Cambridge University Press.

TRUEBA, H. (1983) 'Adjustment problems of Mexican American children: An anthropological study', *Learning Disabilities Quarterly*, **6(4)**, pp. 8–15.

TRUEBA, H. (1985) 'Learning disabilities in La Playa: Ethnographic field notes from 1982 to 1985'. Unpublished manuscript. University of California, Santa Barbara, CA.

TRUEBA, H. (1986) Review of *Beyond Language: Social and Cultural Factors in Schooling Language Minority Students*. In *Anthropology and Education Quarterly*, **17(4)**, pp. 255–59.

TRUEBA, H. (ed.) (1987a) *Success or Failure: Learning and the Language Minority Student*, New York, NY: Newbury House/Harper and Row.

TRUEBA, H. (1987b) 'Ethnography of schooling', in TRUEBA, H. (ed.) *Success or Failure: Linguistic Minority Children at Home and in School*, New York, NY: Harper and Row, pp. 1–13.

TRUEBA, H. (1987c) 'Organizing classroom instruction in specific sociocultural contexts: Teaching Mexican youth to write in English', in GOLDMAN, S. and TRUEBA, H. (eds) *Becoming Literate in English as a Second Language: Advances in Research and Theory*, Norwood, NJ: Ablex Corporation.

TRUEBA, H. (1988a) 'Peer socialization among minority students, A high school dropout prevention program,' in TRUEBA, H. and DELGADO–GAITAN, C. (eds) *School and Society: Learning Content Through Culture*, New York, NY: Praeger Publishers, pp. 201–17.

TRUEBA, H. (1988b) 'English literacy acquisition: From cultural trauma to learning disabilities in minority students' *Linguistics and Education*, **1**, pp. 125–152, 271–287.

TRUEBA, H. (1988c) 'Culturally-based explanations of minority students' academic achievement', *Anthropology and Education Quarterly*, **19(3)**, pp. 270–287.

TRUEBA, H. (1988d) Comments on L. M. Dunn's *Bilingual Hispanic Children on the US Mainland: A Review of Research on Their Cognitive, Linguistic, and Scholastic Development*, in *Hispanic Journal of Behavioral Sciences*, **10(3)**, pp. 253–262.

TRUEBA, H. (1989) *Raising Silent Voices: Educating the Linguistic Minorities for the 21st Century*. New York, NY: Harper and Row.

TRUEBA, H. (1990) 'Rethinking Dropouts: Culture and literacy for minority student empowerment', in TRUEBA, H. and SPINDLER, G. and SPINDLER, L. (eds) *What do Anthropologists have to Say about Dropouts? The First Centennial Conference on Children at Risk*, Basingstoke, England: The Falmer Press, pp. 27–42.

TRUEBA, H. and DELGADO–GAITAN, C. (eds) (1988) *School and Society: Learning Content Through Culture*. New York, NY: Praeger Publishers.

TRUEBA, H., SPINDLER, G. and SPINDLER, L. (eds) (1990) *What do Anthropologists Have to Say about Dropouts?*, Basingstoke, England: The Falmer Press.

TRUEBA, H., MOLL, L., DIAZ, S. and DIAZ, R. (1984) *Improving the Functional Writing of Bilingual Secondary School Students*. (Contract No. 400–81–0023). Washington, DC: National Institute of Education. *ERIC*, Clearinghouse on Languages and Linguistics, ED 240, 862.

U.S. Bureau of the Census (1984) *1980 U.S. Census*. Current Populations Report. Washington DC: Goverment Printing Office.

U.S. Department of Commerce. Bureau of the Census. (1987) *The Hispanic Population in the United States: March 1986 and 1987 (Advance Report)* Washington, DC: U.S. Government Printing Office.

VAN-ES-BEECK, B. (1982) 'Refugees from Laos, 1975–1979', in STUART-FOX, M. (ed.) *Contemporary Laos: Studies in the Politics and Society of the Lao People's Democratic Republic*, New York, NY: St. Martin's Press, pp. 324–34.

VOGT, L., JORDAN, C. and THARP, R. (1987) 'Explaining school failure, producing school success: Two cases', *Anthropology and Education Quarterly*, **18(4)**, pp. 276–86.

VYGOTSKY, L. S. (1962) *Thought and Language*, Cambridge, MA: MIT Press.

VYGOTSKY, L. S. (1978) *Mind in Society: The Development of Higher Psychological Processes*, COLE, M., JOHN-TEINER, V., SCRIBNER, S. and SOUBERMAN, E. (eds), Cambridge, MA: Harvard University Press.

WAGATSUMA, H. and DEVOS, G. (1984) *Heritage of Endurance: Family Patterns and Delinquency Formation in Urban Japan*, Berkeley, CA: University of California Press.

WERNER, O. and SCHOEPHFLE, G. M. (1987) *Systematic Fieldwork. Volume 1: Foundations of Ethnography and Interviewing*, Newbury Park, CA: Sage Publications.

WERNER, O. and SCHOEPHFLE, G. M. (1987) *Systematic Fieldwork. Volume 2: Ethnographic Analysis and Data Management*, Newbury Park, CA: Sage Publications.

WERTSCH, J. (1981) *The Concept of Activity in Soviet Psychology*, New York, NY: M. E. Sharpe, Inc.

WERTSCH, J. (1985) *Vygotsky and the Social Formation of the Mind*, Cambridge, MA: Harvard University Press.

WERTSCH, J. (1987) 'Collective Memory: Issues from a sociohistorical perspective', *The Quarterly Newsletter of the Laboratory of Comparative Human Cognition*, 9(1), pp. 19–22.

WOLCOTT, H. (1987) 'On ethnographic intent', in SPINDLER, G. and L. (1987a) *The Interpretive Ethnography of Education: At Home and Abroad*, Hillsdale, NJ: Lawrence Erlbaum Associates, pp. 37–57.

WOOLCOTT, H. (1988) ' "Problem Finding" in qualitative research', in TRUEBA, H. and DELGADO-GAITAN, C. (eds) *School and Society: Learning Content Through Culture*, New York: Praeger Publishers, pp. 11–35.

XYOOJ, T. (XIONG, C.) (1981) *Phau qhia nyeem tsiaj ntawv hmoob*. Unpublished Hmong primer.

YANG DAO, (1975) *Les Hmong du Laos face au developpement*, Vietiane, Laos: Editions Siosavath.

YANG, DOUA and NORTH, DAVID (1988) *Profiles of the Highland Lao Communities in the United States*, Washington, DC: U.S. Government Printing Office.

YANG, S. and COX, J. W. (1985) *Traditional Tales of the Hmong People*. Unpublished Manuscript. Goleta, CA.

YOUNG, M. (ed.) (1971) *Knowledge and Control: New Directions for the Sociology of Education*, London, England: Collier-Macmillan.

Index